Buses, Coaches & Recollections
Henry Conn

Contents

Title page: **BRISTOL** The last new Bristol KSWs were delivered to Bristol Omnibus between May and October 1957, numbered C8405 to C8431 (YHT 901 to 927). In Park Street, Bristol, on 30 September is No C8415 (YHT 911), an ECW-bodied Bristol KSW6B, which was sold for scrap in October 1973. In the background is the Wills Memorial Building (Wills of tobacco manufacturing fame); begun in 1915 and not opened until 1925, it is considered one of the last great Gothic buildings in England. It is part of the University of Bristol and is the city's third-highest structure at 215 feet. A gallon of petrol on this day would cost you 34p. *Bob Gell*

Acknowledgments

A large number of the illustrations in this book are from the camera of Bob Gell. Without these views and the detailed notes on each, this book would not have been possible. My most sincere thanks to Bob – outstanding!

The PSV Circle Fleet Histories for the operators in this book and a number of issues of *Buses Illustrated* were vital sources of information for this book.

British Library Cataloguing in Publication Data

A catalogue record for this book is available from the British Library.

ISBN 978 1 85794 461 7

Silver Link Publishing Ltd
The Trundle
Ringstead Road
Great Addington
Kettering
Northants NN14 4BW

Tel/Fax: 01536 330588
email: sales@nostalgiacollection.com
Website: www.nostalgiacollection.com

Printed and bound in the Czech Republic

About the author

My first recollections of public transport were early in 1958 in my home town of Aberdeen, travelling from our home in Mastrick to Union Street, then onwards by tram to Bridge of Dee. My interest in buses, trolleybuses and trams expanded to taking fleet numbers or registration numbers, and by the mid-1960s I had acquired a camera and began my collection. This interest continued through my family's moves from Aberdeen to Perth, Whitburn in West Lothian, Banbury, Swindon and Oxford by 1974.

My first job was with Customs & Excise, beginning in London with transfers to Oxford, Dover and Brighton. It was after I left Brighton that my enthusiasm for bus photography waned, and it never really returned apart from sporadic photography when I returned to Scotland in 1980. By this time I had left Customs & Excise and had returned to college in Cupar to study Agriculture. I met my future wife at this college and moved with her parents to Galloway, where I have lived very happily since 1983. To further my career I attended Aberdeen University to take a BSc Degree in Agriculture, and I successfully graduated in 1996. This led to me returning to the Civil Service with the Scottish Executive Rural Affairs Department, then through many changes to where I am now, working with Natural England as adviser to farmers on Environmental Schemes (three days a week from last July).

By 2010 I had a significant collection of transport views from the mid-1960s to the early 1980s. I met with Silver Link Publishing's editor Will Adams in Preston in early 2010 and was very kindly given the opportunity to write a volume on Buses, Trams and Trolleybuses in the Midlands. Since then I have continued to enjoy writing volumes on transport for Silver Link, this volume being my sixth in the 'Recollections' series looking at buses, trolleybuses and trams as well as significant events in a specific year.

Introduction

In 1972 maxi-dresses, mini-skirts, knee socks and patterns happened in a big way. *Grease* had its first Broadway run, spreading far and wide the gospel 'A hickey from Kenickie is like a Hallmark card'. 'Trekkies' rejoiced when the first *Star Trek* fan convention took place in New York City's Statler-Hilton Hotel. David Bowie first introduced his glorious alter ego Ziggy Stardust, and Abba was formed. Atari introduced PONG, which became the first commercially successful video game. The film *Last Tango In Paris* came to cinemas, forever changing the way we looked at a stick of butter. Bill Cosby spoke to kids about drugs … and won a Grammy for it. And holy Augustus Gloop – Roald Dahl's *Charlie and the Great Glass Elevator* was released! Duane 'The Rock' Johnson was born (please take a moment to imagine a baby version of The Rock). Samuel L. Jackson made his movie debut in *Together for Days* and Richard Adams's *Watership Down* was published. Carole King won Record, Album and Song of the Year, while Carly Simon took the Best New Artist award. The best picture award at the Oscars went to *The French Connection*.

The digital watch made its clunky debut in 1972. Aircraft boasted free cocktails for everyone, and very scantily clad stewardesses. Everyone wanted a Volkswagen Beetle, sales of which beat the Model T Ford. I remember the dash to the cinema in Swindon to get tickets to watch Linda Lovelace in *Deep Throat*, the film at the forefront of The Golden Age of Porn.

A draft lottery was held in the United States for the Vietnam War, the last of which to be held. Japan got Okinawa back after it had been controlled by the United States Military for 27 years. The United Kingdom and Iceland engaged in the Second Cod War. In order to distract the people from the collapsing economy, Idi Amin ordered all Asian non-citizens out of the country and confiscated their businesses. In Ireland, 13 protesters were shot by the British Army, touching off riots that led to the suspension of the Northern Ireland parliament. Nike running shoes hit the market, and the first email program was invented by Ray Tomlinson. And Eugene Cernan of Apollo 17 became the last man to walk on the Moon, in December 1972.

Enjoy the nostalgia!

Scotland

ELGIN: Standing in the Northern depot of Walter Alexander & Sons Ltd in Elgin on 17 September is NRB 88 (CWG 66), an Alexander-bodied Leyland PD2/1. This bus was new to Alexander in March 1950 and was transferred to Northern on 15 May 1961; it survived to be exported to the USA in February 1973. *Author's collection*

On this day in the USA the first episode of M*A*S*H premiered on CBS television.

ABERDEEN: Entering Guild Street bus station in Aberdeen on 26 September is NRE 2 (SRS 112), an Alexander-bodied Albion LR1 new to Northern in April 1963. *Author's collection*

On this day a referendum showed that 53.5% of votes cast in Norway rejected membership of the European Economic Community (EEC). On 2 October Denmark voted to join the EEC.

EDINBURGH: Working service 12 to Niddrie on 28 July is No 545 (LWS 545), an MCCW-bodied Leyland PD2/20 new in April 1955; it would be withdrawn and sold for scrap in September 1974. The car standing alongside is a Rover P5B coupé; this was the final model of the Rover P5 range, which had been launched in September 1967. Two models were built, the four-door coupé and saloon, until production ended in 1973, by which time 9,099 coupés and 11,501 saloons had been built. *Author's collection*

EDINBURGH: On 12 September, working service 12, is No 522 (LWS 522), another of the batch of 100 MCCW-bodied Leyland PD2/20s purchased for tram replacement; No 522 was new in March 1955, and would pass to Lothian Regional Transport on 16 May 1975. The overtaking car is a Renault 12, which was introduced to the public at the Paris Motor Show in 1969. *Author's collection*

On the day this view was taken William Boyd died in California, best known for portraying cowboy Hopalong Cassidy on TV in the mid-1950s.

Northern England

BURNLEY: Well remembered for its long-surviving Leyland PS2 half-cabs, this is Burnley, Colne & Nelson's No 44 (CHG 544), a PS2/14 model with East Lancashire bodywork, new in 1954 and seen here on 21 September 1972; it was converted by East Lancashire to front-entrance for one-person operation in November 1957 and remained in the fleet until September 1976. *Author's collection*

This view was taken on the day Liam Gallagher of Oasis was born.

HALIFAX: New as Todmorden No 7 (BWU 689H), a Pennine-bodied Leyland PSU4A/2R, in December 1969, it became No 329 in the Calderdale fleet in September 1971. It is seen here at Halifax depot on 13 April the following year. It became No 3329 in the West Yorkshire PTE fleet and was sold in 1982. The rear of the bus in the depot belongs to Calderdale No 288 (CJX 328C), a Leyland Titan PD2/37 with Weymann bodywork new in December 1965; it passed to West Yorkshire PTE (Calderdale District) in 1974, and was sold to Booth's, Rotherham, for scrap in 1978. *Bob Gell*

Three days after this view was taken, Apollo 16 was launched; the tenth manned mission in the USA Apollo space program, and the fifth and penultimate to land on the Moon, Apollo 16 was the first to land in the lunar highlands.

WAKEFIELD: United Services operated a route from Wakefield to Hemsworth and Doncaster, providing a valuable service to the local mining communities. It was a joint operation by three local operators, Bingley, Cooper Brothers and Everetts. By the time this view was taken in Wakefield bus station on 13 April, the sole operator of United Services was W. R. & P. Bingley of South Elmsall. The bus is AWX 118G, a Plaxton-bodied Leyland PSU3/3R new in 1969. *Bob Gell*

WAKEFIELD:
Between October 1957 and January 1958 West Riding took delivery of Nos 818 to 862 (KHL 818 to 862), Roe-bodied Guy Arab IVs; they were renumbered 421 to 465 in November 1971. They had very well appointed interiors and, partly due to the early demise of the Wulfrunians, had long active service lives, being still in regular all-day service around Castleford and Featherstone in the early 1970s. This is No 423 (KHL 820), also at Wakefield bus station on 13 April; it would be sold for scrap in June 1973. *Bob Gell*

The No 1 single on this day was Amazing Grace performed by The Pipes and Drums and Military Band of The Royal Scots Dragoon Guards.

WAKEFIELD: During 1957 Midland General took delivery of five ECW-bodied Bristol LD6Gs, Nos 459 to 463 (8 to 12 DRB). Between May and September 1970 West Riding acquired all five to help replace the failing Guy Wulfrunians, and 12 DRB, as No 419, is seen here in Wakefield bus station on the same day as the previous views. *Bob Gell*

The No 1 album on this day was the excellent Fog on the Tyne by Lindisfarne, which was followed by the even better Machine Head by Deep Purple.

WAKEFIELD: West Riding bought Bristol RELLs with both Plaxton Derwent and ECW bodywork. Following the company's sale to the National Bus Company (NBC) on 1 January 1969, West Riding switched to ECW for bodywork for its Bristol RE chassis. This is No 314 (WHL 734J), an ECW-bodied example that was new in March 1971. *Bob Gell*

WAKEFIELD: During April and May 1971 West Riding purchased new 12 Alexander-bodied Daimler CRG6LXs (WHL 273J to 284J). About to depart from Wakefield bus station for Dewsbury on that same April day is No 674 (WHL 276J); this bus was acquired by Andrews of Sheffield and was noted in that company's depot at Attercliffe in February 1990. *Bob Gell*

GRIMSBY: On 29 April we see Lincolnshire Road Car No 2241 (NVL 168), an ECW-bodied Bristol MW5G new in January 1960; it would be sold to a dealer in April 1977. *Bob Gell*

On this Saturday I was in Swindon, buying America's single A Horse With No Name – the album came next.

Below **MANCHESTER:** A large number of Burlingham-bodied Leyland PD2/40s were delivered to Manchester Corporation in 1958, and representing this batch is No 3479 (TNA 479); all passed to SELNEC on 1 November 1969. This view of No 3479 was taken in Piccadilly on 3 February. *Author's collection*

This was the first day of the 1972 Winter Olympics in Sapporo.

Above **ROCHDALE:** Heading for Greave in Rochdale on 2 May is No 6203 (ODK 703) of SELNEC (South East Lancashire North East Cheshire PTE; it is a Weymann-bodied AEC Regent V D2RA6G that was new to Rochdale Corporation as its No 303 in 1956. This was one of Rochdale's second batch of Regents with Gardner 6LW engines; these buses had an air-actuated AEC Monocontrol semi-automatic gearbox, while the first batch had an air-actuated preselector gearbox. *Author's collection*

On this day J. Edgar Hoover, Director of the FBI since 1935, died in Washington.

Below **MANCHESTER:** At Manchester Piccadilly station on 27 January, both heading for Wythenshawe and still in Manchester Corporation livery surrounded by orange and white, are SELNEC Nos 4444 and 4465 (NNB 251 and NNB 275), MCCW-bodied Daimler CVG6Ks new in 1954. The 'K' indicates that the rear axle was manufactured by the Kirkstall forge in Leeds; also note the two types of grill, No 4465 with an original and No 4441 with a Manchester Corporation-built replacement. Both buses were sold for scrap in December 1974. *Author's collection*

Born in Oldham on the day this photograph was taken was Mark Owen of Take That.

Above **STALYBRIDGE** The last double-deckers ordered by Stalybridge, Hyde, Mossley & Dukinfield (SHMD) were just that bit different from previous Fleetline deliveries. Ten Daimler CRG6LW's based on Edgeley Cox's 27-foot-long design for Walsall, which featured narrow front entrances and a sliding central exit. They became SELNEC Nos 5638 to 5647 (ELG 38F to 47F); contrast the SELNEC livery of No 5638 (right) with the SHMD livery of No 5644, seen on 13 April at Stalybridge bus station. *Bob Gell*

Right **SHEFFIELD:** In April and May of 1961 the Sheffield Joint Omnibus Committee received five ECW coach-bodied Leyland L1s, 1910 WA to 1914 WA); this is No 1011 (1911 WA) in Pond Street, Sheffield, on 2 September. *Bob Gell*

Four days after this view was taken, at the Sheffield Top Rank Suite, the Ziggy Stardust Tour was fronted by the late, great David Bowie. When the Ziggy Stardust album was released in the beginning of June 1972 the popularity increased enormously. Meanwhile the first UK tour proceeded, a series of larger halls were booked, and the shows started to sell out during the summer of 1972. The tour took a short break, then started up again with the famous show at the Rainbow Theatre in London on 19 August. In August and September the interest in David Bowie continued to grow, and Ziggy hysteria started.

Left **SHEFFIELD:** Working the 76 service to Sheffield Lane Top on 26 August is No 1336 (6336 WJ), one of a batch of 25 Roe-bodied AEC Regent Vs new in early 1960. It is interesting to note that four of them – Nos 1331, 1332, 1336 and 1339 – were still in service in April 1976, and the last, No 1331, completed a full last day in service on 13 May, shuttling back and forth between Sheffield Lane Top and Bradway. *Author's collection*

This was the first day of the Summer Olympics in Munich, which was largely overshadowed by the tragic events of 5 and 6 September.

Right **SHEFFIELD:** To replace the trams on the penultimate route from Meadowhead to Sheffield Lane Top, Sheffield Corporation purchased 26 Weymann-bodied AEC Regent Vs. This view of No 444 (7444 WJ) was taken on 13 May 1972; it was unusual to find an ageing AEC Regent V on the 37 service to Bakewell in the Peak District in this year. The car behind No 444 is an early Sunbeam Alpine. *Author's collection*

On this day actor Dan Blocker died at the age of 43. He was best known for his role as 'Hoss' Cartwright in TV's *Bonanza*, which ran from 1959 to 1972; only one series was completed after his death.

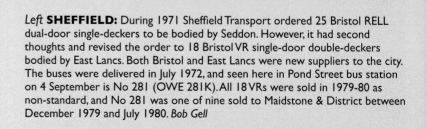

Left **SHEFFIELD:** During 1971 Sheffield Transport ordered 25 Bristol RELL dual-door single-deckers to be bodied by Seddon. However, it had second thoughts and revised the order to 18 Bristol VR single-door double-deckers bodied by East Lancs. Both Bristol and East Lancs were new suppliers to the city. The buses were delivered in July 1972, and seen here in Pond Street bus station on 4 September is No 281 (OWE 281K). All 18 VRs were sold in 1979-80 as non-standard, and No 281 was one of nine sold to Maidstone & District between December 1979 and July 1980. *Bob Gell*

Below **SHEFFIELD:** Standing in Pond Street is No 1293 (YWB 293), an ECW-bodied Leyland PD2/20 new in July 1957. The ECW bodywork looks similar to those fitted to the Bristol KSW, but with deeper sliders, and is in my opinion a good-looking and well-proportioned 'tin-fronted' bus. Standing alongside, in comparison, is No 947 (947 BWB), a Roe-bodied Leyland PDR1/1 new in April 1962. *Bob Gell*

Above **SHEFFIELD:** During April and May 1971 Sheffield took delivery of 30 Park Royal dual-doorway Daimler CRG6LXs, Nos 682 to 711 (HWJ 682J to 711J). Representing the batch on 4 September is No 693 (HWJ 693J). *Bob Gell*

One of my favourite songs was in the Top 10 in the USA singles charts at this time, Long Tall Woman in a Black Dress by the Hollies. With its great guitar intro, bass vocals and lyric, put it on full blast when driving and you'll be tapping away as soon as it starts!

1972 No 1 Records

January
New Seekers   *I'd Like to Teach the World to Sing*

February
T. Rex   *Telegraph Sam*
Chicory Tip   *Son of my Father*

March
Nilsson   *Without You*

April
Pipes and Drums and Military Band of the Royal
Scots Dragoon Guards   *Amazing Grace*

May
T. Rex   *Metal Guru*

June
Don McLean   *Vincent*

July
Slade   *Take Me Bak 'Ome*
Donny Osmond   *Puppy Love*

August
Alice Cooper   *School's Out*

September
Rod Stewart   *You Wear It Well*
Slade   *Mama Weer All Crazee Now*

October
Lieutenant Pigeon   *Mouldy Old Dough*

November
Gilbert O'Sullivan   *Clair*
Chuck Berry   *My Ding-a-Ling*

December
Little Jimmy Osmond   *Long Haired Lover From
                                                    Liverpool*

LINCOLN: Photographed on 29 April , this is Lincoln Corporation No 78 (KVL 682), a Roe-bodied Leyland PD2/31, one of six new in September 1957. *Bob Gell*

On this day England lost to West Germany 3-1 in the European Championship; the England scorer was Franny Lee.

Photo	DESTINATIONS
	EAST MIDLANDS
25	MANSFIELD
26	NEWARK
27	NEWARK
28	UNDERWOOD
29	BULWELL
30	NOTTINGHAM
31	NOTTINGHAM
32	NOTTINGHAM
33	NOTTINGHAM
34	NOTTINGHAM
35	DERBY
36	BURTON UPON TRENT
37	BURTON UPON TRENT
	WEST MIDLANDS
38	HEATH HAYES
38	HEATH HAYES
39	HEATH HAYES
40	CANNOCK
41	WALSALL
42	WALSALL

East Midlands

MANSFIELD: In July 1971 East Midland took delivery of five Alexander-bodied Leyland PDR1/3s, Nos D196 to D200 (CRR 196J to 200J), and standing on the forecourt of the East Midland depot at Westgate in Mansfield on 2 September is the first of them. *Bob Gell*

Three days earlier, Cameron Diaz was born in San Diego, California.

Right **NEWARK:** Mansfield & District took delivery of three ECW-bodied Bristol VRT/SL6Gs in July 1970, Nos 323 to 325 (FRB 212H to 214H), and seen here in Newark bus station about to depart for Mansfield on 4 June is No 325. Behind it is Lincolnshire Road Car No 2259 (AVL 741C), an ECW-bodied Bristol MW6G new in May 1965. *Bob Gell*

Left **NEWARK:** Photographed at the bus station on the same day, en route to Skegness, is Trent No 15 (VCH 15G), a Plaxton-bodied Leyland PSU3A/4R new in March 1969. Behind it, working Gash's direct service to Nottingham is TVO 981G, a Plaxton-bodied Leyland PSU4/3R new to Gash in January 1969. On the right, the ECW-bodied Bristol FS5G is OVL 475, which was new to Lincolnshire Road Car in July 1960 and would remain in its fleet until sold for scrap in April 1978. *Bob Gell*

A few days earlier, at Bardney in Lincolnshire, The Great Western Festival took place with music provided by Rory Gallagher on 26 May, Wishbone Ash, Roxy Music, Nazareth and The Faces on the 27th, The Beach Boys, Lindisfarne, Slade and Focus on the 28th, and on the final day Genesis, Don McLean, Atomic Rooster and Status Quo – fantastic!

Above **UNDERWOOD:** Delivered to Midland General in October 1969, this is No 319 (DRB 308H), an ECW-bodied Bristol VRT/SL6G, seen at Underwood, near Eastwood, Nottinghamshire, on 20 August. *Bob Gell*

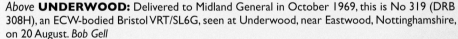

On this day School's Out by Alice Cooper was the No 1 single, and if you did not like that anthem there was Silver Machine by Hawkwind, Layla by Derek and the Dominoes, I Can See Clearly Now by Johnny Nash, Sylvia's Mother by Dr Hook and Virginia Plain by Roxy Music, all selling well in the charts.

Top Right **BULWELL:** Crossing the railway at Carey Road in Bulwell, north of Nottingham, on 20 January is Nottingham Corporation No 148 (MTO 148F), one of a batch of 35 NCME-bodied Daimler CRG6LXs new between November 1967 and February 1968. No 148 itself was new in December 1967, and was rebuilt to dual-doorway form by Seddon in November 1969 (all the batch were so treated). This former Midland Railway line is now known as the 'Robin Hood Line' between Nottingham and Worksop, and is shared with the Nottingham Express Transit trams to Hucknall. *Bob Gell*

At this time UK unemployment exceeded 1 million for the first time since the Second World War.

Above **NOTTINGHAM:** Leaving the city's Victoria bus station for Southwell on 11 November is Mansfield & District No A273 (271 HNU), an ECW-bodied Bristol MW6G that was new to Midland General in 1959. *Bob Gell*

By the beginning of 1972 more than 400,000 US personnel had been withdrawn from Vietnam, virtually all combat troops. On this day the massive Long Binh military base, once the largest US installation outside the USA, was handed over to the South Vietnamese.

NOTTINGHAM: Corporation took delivery of 35 Weymann-bodied AEC Renowns between April and June 1965, and this is No 376 (DAU 376C) in Bilborough Road, Nottingham, on 14 October. No 376 was withdrawn and sold to Kirby's Coaches, Bushey Heath, in January 1977, remained there until sold for scrap in February 1980. *Bob Gell*

The day before this view was taken a Uruguayan Air Force passenger aircraft transporting a rugby union team crashed 14,000 feet up in the Andes. Sixteen survivors were found alive on 20 December, but they had been forced to resort to cannibalism to survive. The film Alive *released in 1993 told the harrowing story.*

Below **NOTTINGHAM:** In Mount Street parking area on 3 June is Barton No 1191 (GAL 24J), a Plaxton-bodied Leyland PSU3B/4R new in June 1971; it would be sold to Morris of Pencoed after just five years with Barton, then two years later it passed to Bedminster Coaches in Bristol, and was still owned by that company in February 1984. *Bob Gell*

On this day Nottinghamshire beat Yorkshire in the Benson & Hedges Cup at Trent Bridge.

Top Right **NOTTINGHAM:** Hall Brothers of South Shields was purchased by Barton in July 1967, but continued as a wholly owned subsidiary until the vehicles were progressively transferred to Barton between 1969 and 1971. No 1174 (ECU 755E) was new to Hall Brothers in May 1967 and is seen here on 3 June outside the Barton depot opposite Huntingdon Street bus station in Nottingham. It was one of the last to be transferred from Hall's to Barton in January 1971, and after withdrawal by Barton in 1974 the coach passed to J. T. Waites of Altrincham, Lester of Norbury and finally Great Wyrley High School in 1982. *Bob Gell*

On this day in Northern Ireland a Protestant march against the creation of no-go areas in Londonderry ended in a bitter battle between marchers and soldiers on the Craigavon Bridge.

Above **NOTTINGHAM:** Leaving Huntingdon Street bus station on the same day is Lancashire United No 198 (LTB 307C), a Plaxton-bodied Leyland L2 new in March 1965. The X92 (Saturdays only) started in Liverpool and ran to Nottingham jointly with Trent. Then, as a through coach, as seen here on hire to Trent, it ran as the X7 from Nottingham to Great Yarmouth. *Bob Gell*

Left **NOTTINGHAM:** During October 1972 Nottingham took on loan four new Leyland Nationals from London Country, Nos LN8 to LN11 (NPD 108L to 111L), and they operated a free Central Area Service in Nottingham until August 1973, when the city's own Leyland Nationals were delivered. This is NPD 111L in South Sherwood Street on 11 November. Nos LN8, 10 and 11 would never enter service with London Country and passed to Hants & Dorset in September 1973 in exchange for ex-King Alfred Metro-Scanias AOU 108J to AOU 110J. *Bob Gell*

Johnny Nash's I Can See Clearly Now *was No 1 on this day, and would chart again in 1993 when it was featured on the Walt Disney film* Cool Runnings.

Right **DERBY:** At Westmore Park bus station on 11 March is Blue Bus Services' NRA 49J, an Alexander-bodied Daimler CRG6LX new in May 1971. The business of Tailby & George Ltd (Blue Bus Services) later passed to Derby City Transport on 21 December 1973, and this bus would be destroyed by fire at Willington depot on 5 January 1979. Victoria Motorways of Woodville purchased new three Willowbrook-bodied Ford R192s (OFA 917H to 919H), and on the left, representing this batch, is OFA 917H. Just visible on the right is Trent No 625 (625 CCH), a Northern Counties-bodied Daimler CRG6LX new in 1963. *Bob Gell*

Carnival Cruise Lines made its very first voyage when the Mardi Gras departed from Miami for an eight-day cruise, and ran aground on a sandbar. The 530 passengers, most of whom were travel agents and their families, continued to enjoy themselves until tugboats dislodged the ship the next day, and the new company received national publicity from the incident.

Below **BURTON UPON TRENT:** At the bus station on 11 March is No 2 (NLJ 272), a Burlingham-bodied Leyland PSU1/13 that was new to Bournemouth Corporation in February 1954. It originally had dual doorways but was rebuilt to front doorway only and one-person operation by Bournemouth in 1960. Burton acquired the bus in May 1971 and it entered service a month later. Withdrawn in July 1976, it was acquired by Bournemouth Passenger Transport Association in April 1977 for preservation. *Bob Gell*

Films released the day before this view was taken were **Silent Running** *with Bruce Dern and* **What's Up, Doc?** *with Ryan O'Neal and Barbra Streisand.*

Above **BURTON UPON TRENT:** Between February 1962 and January 1968 Burton Corporation purchased new 34 Massey-bodied Daimler CCG5s, a model that had a Gardner 5LW engine with a Guy four-speed crash gearbox. This is No 82 (SFA 82), which was new in March 1963 and was acquired by J. Stevenson of Uttoxeter in August 1973, remaining in that fleet until sold for scrap in July 1977. *Bob Gell*

The Billboard No 1 single on 11 March was the lovely **Without You** *by Harry Nilsson.*

West Midlands

Right **HEATH HAYES:** During 1963 Guy Motors of Wolverhampton took delivery of 888 DUK, a Strachan-bodied Guy Arab V demonstrator. After visiting a number of operators, including Halifax and Great Yarmouth Corporations, the vehicle was acquired by Harper Brothers of Heath Hayes, near Cannock, in May 1966. It is seen here passing Harpers' depot at Heath Hayes on 11 March in the operator's unusual livery. Harper Brothers' vehicles passed to Midland Red on 7 September 1974 and 888 DUK operated with its new owner for little over a month before being damaged in an accident; it had been scrapped by July 1975. *Bob Gell*

Below **HEATH HAYES:** Glimpsed on the right of the previous picture, on the parking area in front of Harper Brothers' Heath Hayes depot, was No 60 (1294 RE), a Guy Arab LUF with Burlingham Seagull bodywork new in July 1959. This vehicle passed to Midland Red on 7 September 1974 and was subsequently sold into preservation. *Bob Gell*

Below **HEATH HAYES:** Also present on that day was No 22 (1031 E). New to Harper Brothers in May 1953 with C41C Burlingham bodywork, the coach was re-styled and re-seated to DP41F and fitted for one-person operation in 1968. It also passed to Midland Red on 7 September 1974, and was sold for scrap in April 1975. *Bob Gell*

Right **CANNOCK:** Two Daimler CRG6LXs with Northern Counties bodywork, Nos 29 and 30 (JBF 405H and 406H), were purchased new by Harpers Brothers in May 1970, and again both passed to Midland Red with Harpers' business on 7 September 1974. They were fitted for one-person operation in September 1974 and passed to Midland Red (North) Limited, Cannock, on 6 September 1981, at the formation of that company. They were both withdrawn in September 1983 and sold for scrap in March 1984. No 29 is seen at Cannock bus station on 11 March. *Bob Gell*

Four days later **The Godfather,** *directed by Francis Ford Coppola, debuted in five cinemas in New York and until 1975 would hold the record for the highest grossing film in history, taking $87.5 million in its first release.*

Below **WALSALL:** A demonstration Alexander-bodied Daimler CRG6LX, 565 CRW, was borrowed by West Bromwich Corporation between 14 March and 3 April 1965, and as a result of the trials the Corporation ordered 14 MCW-bodied examples. The first was completely destroyed by fire, and the remaining 13, delivered in May 1967, were numbered 102 to 114 (KEA 102E to 114E). The bodywork was built to a lower height, noticeable by the reduced height of the lower saloon windows. Standing in Walsall bus station on 11 March, still in West Bromwich low-height livery, is WMPTE No 102 (KEA 102E); it was sold for scrap in March 1983. *Bob Gell*

The No 1 album on this day was **Harvest** *by Neil Young, and one of the featured songs was the excellent* **Heart of Gold.**

Left **WALSALL:** The first reverse registration marks for West Bromwich were issued in March 1960, and the operator's first buses to feature them were Nos 228 to 232 (228 to 232 DEA), Metro-Cammell-bodied Daimler CVG6s that entered service on 22 December of that year. Now in West Midlands PTE livery, 232 DEA is seen in Walsall bus station on 11 March 1972. During the year 27 former West Bromwich buses were transferred to Walsall to replace older Birmingham and Walsall buses. Nos 228 to 232 would be sold for scrap in January 1975. *Bob Gell*

Wales

LLANDUDNO: Bristol introduced its lightweight front-engine SC chassis in 1954 and, despite only having a four-cylinder engine, Crosville was one of the biggest customers. Working a local service in Llandudno on 13 July is No SSG 628 (569 JFM), an ECW-bodied Bristol SC4LK new in March 1959. It was sold on in October 1975, and between September 1977 and late 1979 it was in the fleet of Yorkshire Egg Producers of Wardle as staff transport, before being sold for scrap in January 1980. *Author's collection*

On this day the House of Commons narrowly approved the UK's entry into the EEC, voting 301 to 284.

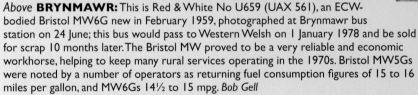

Above **BRYNMAWR:** This is Red & White No U659 (UAX 561), an ECW-bodied Bristol MW6G new in February 1959, photographed at Brynmawr bus station on 24 June; this bus would pass to Western Welsh on 1 January 1978 and be sold for scrap 10 months later. The Bristol MW proved to be a very reliable and economic workhorse, helping to keep many rural services operating in the 1970s. Bristol MW5Gs were noted by a number of operators as returning fuel consumption figures of 15 to 16 miles per gallon, and MW6Gs 14½ to 15 mpg. *Bob Gell*

Top Right **ABERBEEG:** Nearest the camera on the same day is Jones of Aberbeeg No 116 (146 GAX), a Plaxton-bodied AEC Reliance new in April 1963. Behind it, heading for Abertillery, is No 110 (98 EAX), a Willowbrook-bodied AEC Reliance new in 1962. Both buses were sold for scrap in September 1976. *Bob Gell*

The day before this view was taken, US President Richard Nixon and White House Chief of Staff H. R. Haldeman were taped talking about using the CIA to obstruct the FBI's investigation into the Watergate break-ins.

Right **ABERBEEG:** On the same day we see Jones's No 21 (OWO 755F), a Willowbrook-bodied Leyland PSUC1/12 new in 1968; this bus would be sold for scrap in December 1980. *Bob Gell*

The next day, 25 June, Slade were at No 1 in the charts with Take Me Bak 'Ome, but for one week only – for the next five weeks it was Donny Osmond with Puppy Love. I have to say I did not buy these singles!

Right **CROSSKEYS:** Between May and June 1969 Western Welsh took delivery of 20 Marshall-bodied Leyland PSU3A/4Rs, Nos 619 to 638 (PKG 619G to 638G). At the Western Welsh depot in Crosskeys on 24 June, nearest the camera is No 625 (PKG 625G); all but one of the batch were sold for scrap in late 1980 after only 11 years of service. *Bob Gell*

On 12 June Her Royal Highness Princess Anne officially opened the National Sports Centre for Wales (which had opened for sports the previous year).

Below Right **NEWPORT:** Two Metro-Scania BR111MHs, VWD 451H and 452H, with MCW bodywork were built as demonstrators in 1969, and one was demonstrated in Newport. As a result Newport Corporation purchased 44 of them between 1971 and 1972. With their fully automatic gearboxes and light power steering, they were well suited to the Corporation's new style of one-person operation, and were popular with the large number of women bus conductors who were retrained to become drivers; by the end of 1972 15% of the undertaking's drivers were women. Maintenance staff were sent to Sweden on training courses, and after various teething troubles were resolved the buses settled in to become the backbone of Newport's fleet. The following year Newport was offered six 1973 Metro-Scania single-deckers that had been used for a relatively short time by London Transport, and bought them as suitable for spare parts. The package cost £10,000, but the buses were found to be in much better condition than expected, and four were placed back in service. Leaving Newport bus station on 22 April is one of them, No 22 (VDW 422K). *Bob Gell*

South West England and the West Country

CHEPSTOW's Town Gate was historically the only landward entrance to the town through the Port Wall, and a point where tolls for its market were collected. It was originally built, with the wall, in the late 13th century, but the current archway mainly dates from the 16th century, and has been restored and partly rebuilt on several occasions. It is located at the western end of the town's High Street, and is a Grade I listed building. Passing through it on 24 June is Red & White No L263 (164 HAX), an ECW-bodied Bristol FS6G new in 1963. *Bob Gell*

CHELTENHAM: Standing in the Royal Well bus station on 22 April is 41 SAU of Castleways of Winchcombe This coach had been new to Skills of Nottingham in May 1963 and was sold in May 1966 to Foley of Cranford. By April 1968 it was in the fleet of Chumbley, of Brimington, Chesterfield. In September 1971 Castleways acquired it and retained it in the fleet until October 1973. The next owner was Carnell of Sutton Bridge, which kept it for a year before selling it to Young of Rampton, near Cambridge, and after eight months it was sold on again to Barwell Rubber of Swavesey. *Bob Gell*

In the USA anti-war demonstrations drew 100,000 protestors in cities across the USA, including New York, San Francisco, Los Angeles and Chicago.

Right **CHELTENHAM:** Standing in Cheltenham coach station on the same day is 140 DBO, a Duple Northern Alpine Continental-bodied Leyland PSU3/3RT new to Western Welsh in April 1963 and sold to Black & White Motorways of Cheltenham in September 1971. This livery application was adopted by a number of National Bus Company operators in the South West just before the corporate livery was imposed, each company using the major colour of its livery as the contrast. The coach passed to Wessex National in November 1974 and was sold to Creamline Services, Tonmawr, in March 1976, which sold it for scrap in October 1979. *Bob Gell*

Below **CHELTENHAM:** Leaving the coach station for Norwich, also on 22 April, is Eastern Counties' No RE 858 (CAH 858K), a Bristol RELH6G with a Plaxton Panorama Elite body new in 1971; it carries a very early example of the National white livery. *Bob Gell*

GLOUCESTER: New to Bristol Omnibus in February 1962 was No 7033 (201 NAE), an ECW-bodied Bristol FLF6B. Between May 1972 and April 1974 the bus carried an all-over advertising livery for Berni Inns, as seen in this view taken on 14 June in London Road, Gloucester. The bus is working the frequent service 549 between Gloucester and Cheltenham. *Bob Gell*

*At the movies you could be watching **Deliverance** with Burt Reynolds, Jon Voight and Ronny Cox.*

CHELTENHAM: On 19 August, working a summer Saturday duplicate, is 100 VAL of Torrs Coaches, Nottingham. This coach had been new to Brumpton of Dunham-on-Trent in March 1964. *Bob Gell*

Between 14 and 23 June Hurricane Agnes killed 117 on the US East Coast.

GLOUCESTER: XHW 413, an ECW-bodied Bristol LS5G, entered service with Bristol as No 2897 in February 1957. A year later it was working out of Stroud depot, and was equipped for one-person operation in December 1958. In December 1963 it was transferred to Lawrence Hill depot, and two years later to Bath Tramways. After three years at Lawrence Hill it moved to Trowbridge for country services. In October 1971 No 2987 was rebuilt as an LS6G, receiving new flat rubber-mounted windscreens, and transferred to Gloucester with a new fleet number 3002. This view of No 3002 was taken at Gloucester depot on 14 June. The bus ended up with a service life of more than 20 years before being sold for scrap In January 1978. *Bob Gell*

1972 Happenings (1)

January
Kurt Waldheim becomes UN Secretary-General
First scientific hand-held calculator introduced
First woman judge at Old Bailey in London
RMS *Queen Elizabeth* destroyed by fire in Hong Kong harbour
Japanese soldier discovered in Guam, having spent 28 years in jungle
Bloody Sunday: Army kills 14 unarmed nationalist civil rights marchers in Northern Ireland

February
Anti-British riots throughout Ireland
Winter Olympics held in Sapporo, Japan
Mariner 9 sends pictures as it orbits Mars
Strike by miners leads to Government declaring state of emergency
US President Nixon makes unprecedented eight-day visit to China

March
Pioneer 10 launched from Cape Kennedy, first man-made satellite to leave solar system
Government introduces 'Direct Rule' in Northern Ireland and suspends Parliament there
Bradford trolleybus system, last in UK, closes

April
US, USSR and some 70 nations sign Convention banning biological warfare
During Apollo 16 mission, a lunar rover speed record of 18kmph is made
Lockheed L-1011 TriStar enters service
Genocide against Hutu people in Burundi; more than 500,000 Hutus die

Right **SWINDON:** Three Weymann-bodied Daimler CVs were delivered to Swindon in April 1960, fitted with Daimler engines and numbered 112 to 114 (UMR 112 to 114). Standing in the Corporation depot on 14 June is No 114; it passed to Thamesdown Transport on 1 April 1974 and remained in that fleet until October 1977, when it was sold for scrap. *Bob Gell*

I was living in Swindon at this time and the movie on at the Odeon at Regent Circus was Frenzy, an Alfred Hitchcock thriller with Jon Finch. The other cinema I remember in 1972 was the ABC in Regent Street.

Left **BRISTOL:** GGM 431D was the prototype of the Bristol VR chassis and was exhibited at the Commercial Motor Show of 1966. Its Gardner LX engine was mounted longitudinally on the offside, behind the rear axle, making it a VRL rather than VRT (for 'Transverse'). It was first demonstrated to the Scottish Bus Group and entered the fleet of Central SMT in January 1967 as No BN331. In May 1970 it passed to Bristol Omnibus and entered service as No C5000 in September 1970. However, it proved unpopular and troublesome and was withdrawn from service in September 1973. Sold to dealers North, then Ensign, it was acquired by Osborne of Tollesbury, becoming No 29 and remaining in that fleet until December 1986. Unfortunately, this unique bus was scrapped in March 1991. This view of No C5000 was taken at Lawrence Hill, Bristol, on 13 June. *Bob Gell*

The Ziggy Stardust Tour with David Bowie was at Colston Hall, Bristol, on this night.

BRISTOL: This is Bristol Omnibus No C7133 (826 SHW), an ECW-bodied Bristol FLF6G new in March 1964. It received a cream and green livery in May 1971 as a prototype for the new double-deck fleet, but a month later the green areas were repainted in London Country 'Lincoln Green' livery using paint in stock for the repainting of ex-South Wales AEC Swifts, which Bristol Omnibus was repainting at the time for London Country. This unique livery is seen here at Lawrence Hill on the same day as the previous picture. No C7133 was sold by a dealer to Broadbent Motors, Stamford Bridge, in September 1979, and was scrapped in March 1983. *Bob Gell*

SOUTHAMPTON: On service 13 passing Tommy Whites restaurant on 19 August is No 355 (375 FCR), an East Lancashire-bodied AEC Regent V new in November 1973; it would be sold for scrap in August 1979. *Author's collection*

On this day the Canberra and Oriana were berthed in Southampton docks. The Canberra sailed between the UK and Australia for many years, and in 1974 was adapted for cruising; in 1982 she became a troop ship for the invasion of the Falkland Islands.

EXETER: The Bristol LHS was a small lightweight chassis specifically designed for rural routes, and was a good choice for the narrow Devon lanes; six Marshall-bodied examples were ordered by Devon General before the company was absorbed by the National Bus Company. Numbered 88 to 93 (VOD 88K to 93K), all entered service in February 1972, and this view of No 91 was taken at Exeter bus station on 23 April. The Harrington-bodied AEC Reliance on the left, DAF 100C, belongs to Hawkey of Newquay. *Bob Gell*

In a referendum in France on this day, voters approved the treaty adding the UK, Ireland and Denmark to the Common Market, with more than 68% in favour.

1972 Happenings (2)

May

Large-scale US bombing operations against North Vietnam continue

Okinawa returned to Japan after 27 years of US occupation

Governor George C. Wallace of Alabama shot and paralysed at political rally

Ceylon becomes republic of Sri Lanka

Rangers win UEFA Cup Winners' Cup, beating FC Dynamo Moscow 3-2, but pitch invasion means team is banned from defending trophy the following season

June

In Vietnam, Associated Press photographer takes Pulitzer Prize-winning photograph of naked child running down road after being burned by napalm

Watergate scandal – five White House operatives arrested for breaking into offices of Democratic National Committee

West Germany beats Soviet Union 3-0 to win Euro 72

Computer firm Atari founded

July

On 'Bloody Friday' 22 Provisional IRA bombs explode in Belfast

US launches *Landsat 1*, first Earth-resources satellite

National docks strike in UK

'Troubles' escalate in Northern Ireland

EXETER: In the bus station on 23 September is Devon General No 549 (VOD 549K), an ECW-bodied Bristol VRT/SL2 new in August 1971. *Bob Gell*

On 14 September the first episode of **The Waltons** *was broadcast on CBS; the series ran for ten seasons.*

PLYMOUTH: This impressive line-up of Metro-Cammell-bodied Leyland PDR1/1s was photographed at Milehouse depot on 23 April. Nearest the camera is No 137 (TCO 537), which was new in June 1960; it was withdrawn from service in January 1976 and became a training bus until October 1983. It was then used as an enquiry office and later the drivers'/inspectors' control vehicle in the city centre before being eventually sold to a dealer in Exeter in April 1989. Four months later it was sold into preservation. *Bob Gell*

Six days later the Ziggy Stardust Tour had reached the Guild Hall in Plymouth.

London

VICTORIA COACH STATION:

The BMMO CM6 and CM6T was a successful design, but still had a very short service life compared with other BMMO vehicles. High mileage was part of the reason for this, and certain unique parts became difficult to find after BMMO vehicle production ceased in 1970. Another issue was corrosion, as road spray containing salt was a major problem with these vehicles due to their heavy motorway mileages, and the CM6 had no corrosion protection. All of the CM6 coaches were withdrawn with less than 10 years service. On the right of this view taken on 23 September is No 5653 (BHA 653C), new in May 1965. In the centre is No 5668 (EHA 668D), new in March 1966, while on the left, contrasting with the two red-liveried Midland Red CM6s, is National Bus Company-liveried CM6 No 5658 (BHA 658C), which was new in October 1965. All three were withdrawn in April 1974 and scrapped by the end of the year. *Bob Gell*

VICTORIA COACH STATION: By the mid-1960s Ribble was looking for a replacement for its Leyland Atlantean coaches; in 1966 Bristol introduced its rear-engine VRL, and the prototype ECW-bodied VRL appeared at the 1968 Earls Court Motor Show, entering service during December of that year. The prototype VRL, FCK 450G, was powered by the Power Plus Leyland 0.680 engine producing 175bhp at 2,000rpm; the drive was via a five-speed semi-automatic gearbox and there was power steering. Ribble was happy with the prototype and purchased a further 29 production VRLs between 1970 and 1972; these differed from the prototype in that the fuel tanks were on the near side of the chassis, there were no wheel trims, and the window in the luggage locker door was not fitted.

During February and March 1971 Standerwick took delivery of 11 ECW-bodied Bristol VRL/LH6Ls, Nos 51 to 61 (LRN 51J to 61J), and having just arrived

at Victoria on the same day as the previous picture is No 59 (LRN 59J). The VRLs were used on the company's London services from Blackpool, East Lancashire and Southport. It is well known that the buses were troublesome in service, the main problem being the complex driveline from the gearbox to the rear axle. By 1977 all the VRLs had been withdrawn and replaced by Leyland Leopards. *Bob Gell*

1972 Happenings (3)

August
> Dictator Idi Amin declares that Uganda will expel 50,000 Asians with British passports to Britain within three months
> Summer Olympics held in Munich, West Germany

September
> Bobby Fischer defeats Boris Spassky to became first US world chess champion
> Second Cod War begins between UK and Iceland
> First episode of *The Price Is Right* aired on US TV
> Eleven Israeli athletes murdered at Olympics in Munich by terrorist group Black September
> Brazilian driver Emerson Fittipaldi becomes youngest Formula 1 World Champion
> TV series *M*A*S*H* begins its run on CBS

October
> Alex Comfort's best-selling manual *The Joy of Sex* is published
> Rioting by Maze Prison inmates causes fire that destroys most of camp
> After visit to South Vietnam, US National Security Advisor Henry Kissinger suggests that 'peace is at hand'
> Airbus A300 makes first flight

VICTORIA COACH STATION: The attractive coach on the left of this view from the same September day is MJG 49, one of dozen Beadle coach-bodied AEC Reliances that were new to East Kent between March and June 1957. All would have long service lives, most surviving until 1975, and MJG 49 would be sold for scrap in September 1976. The other coach is Black & White No 322 (YDF 322K), a Plaxton-bodied Leyland PSU3B/4R, only a month into service when this view was taken. *Bob Gell*

Five days earlier a diplomat at the Israeli embassy in London was killed by a letter bomb. Eight bombs were addressed to diplomats at the embassy, but three were detected in the consulate's post room and four others were intercepted at a sorting office in Earl's Court. Fifty-one letter bombs in total were sent on 16 September from Amsterdam to Israeli embassies all over the world, but the diplomat in London was the only fatality.

HARROW WEALD: Working out of London Transport's Harrow Weald depot on a 140 service to Heathrow on 16 October is No RT3812 (NXP 819), which had entered service with London Country in October 1953 at Southall depot and had soon been transferred to Crawley. In November 1965, after overhaul at Aldenham and the fitting of a Park Royal body, RT3812 was transferred to the London Transport depot at Harrow Weald, where it remained until November 1972, when it was transferred to the training fleet; it was sold for scrap in April 1976. The H-registration sports car beside the bus is a Jensen Interceptor; a total of just over 6,400 were produced between 1966 and 1976. *Author's collection*

On this day the first episode of Emmerdale Farm was broadcast, and British-born actor Leo Carroll, best known for his role as Alexander Waverly in TV's The Man from UNCLE, died in Hollywood.

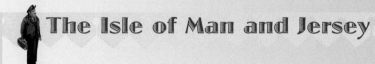

The Isle of Man and Jersey

DOUGLAS: During 1949 Douglas Corporation took delivery of eight Northern Counties-bodied AEC Regent IIIs, Nos 64 to 71 (KMN 835 to 842), and leaving the Isle of Man sea terminal on 23 June is No 68 (KMN 839). In the background is the restaurant on the top floor, known as the 'Crow's Nest'; it was quite popular as it boasted views over the main harbour, but is now used as the harbour control unit. *Author's collection*

On this day footballer/manager Zinedine Zidane was born in Marseille, France.

ST HELIER: Leaving Weighbridge bus station for Plemont, on the north side of the island, and the location of what is probably Jersey's most beautiful beach, is JMT No 612 (J 26612), a Massey-bodied Leyland PSUC1/11 new in 1961. *Bob Gell*

ST HELIER: Following the relaxation of the width limits on Jersey to permit the operation of 8-foot-wide buses, Trimdon Motor Services transferred a number of Plaxton Derwent-bodied Ford R192s. Originally registered VUP 147F, this is JMT No 38 (J 4556) on 5 August.

Two days after this view was taken Geri Halliwell of Spice Girls fame was born in Watford.

1972 Happenings (4)

November

Atari launches arcade version of commercially successful computer game 'Pong'

In US Presidential elections Richard Nixon scores landslide victory over George McGovern

'Tea house' 'Mellow Yellow' opens in Amsterdam, pioneering legal sale of cannabis in the Netherlands

December

Apollo 17 makes final Moon landing, concluding US program of lunar exploration

International Human Rights Day proclaimed by UN

East and West Germany recognise each other

Christmas bombing of North Vietnam causes widespread criticism of US and President Nixon

ST AUBINS BAY: On 4 August we see JMT No 16 (J 1583), a Reading-bodied Leyland PD2/31 new in 1958. The green and cream livery, which had been used for many years, began to be replaced by a blue and cream livery from 1971 when JMT was purchased by Trimdon Motor Services. In the background is one of JMT's eight former London Transport RTLs. *Bob Gell*

1972 Arrivals

Name	Occupation	Date
Claudia Winkelman	TV presenter	15 January
Mark Owen	Musician	27 January
Dana International	Israeli transsexual singer	2 February
Steve McManaman	Footballer	11 February
Billie Joe Armstrong	Musician (Green Day)	17 February
Michael Chang	US tennis player	22 February
Darren Anderton	Footballer	3 March
Jos Verstappen	Racing driver	5 March
Jimmy Floyd Hasselbaink	Footballer	27 March
Nick Frost	Comedy actor	28 March
Jennifer Garner	Actress	17 April
Rivaldo	Footballer	19 April
Dwayne Johnson	US wrestler and actor	2 May
Richard Blackwood	Comedian, actor and rapper	15 May
Buster Rhymes	Rapper and actor	20 May
Rubens Barrichello	Racing driver	23 May
Zinedine Zidane	Footballer	23 June
Marlon Wayans	Actor, comedian and producer	23 July
Wil Wheaton	Actor	29 July
Geri Halliwell	Singer	6 August
Ben Affleck	Actor	15 August
Mikey Graham	Singer (Boyzone)	15 August
Frankie Boyle	Comedian	16 August
Cameron Diaz	Actress	30 August
Natasha Kaplinsky	Newsreader	9 September
Jimmy Carr	Comedian	15 September
Liam Gallagher	Musician	21 September
Karl Pilkington	Radio producer	23 September
Gwyneth Paltrow	Actress	27 September
Robert Webb	Comedian and actor	29 September
Marshall Mathers (Eminem)	Rapper and actor	17 October
Matt Dawson	Rugby player	31 October
Samantha Womack	Actress	2 November
Thandie Newton	Actress	6 November
Miranda Hart	Comedian and actress	14 December
Shane Meadows	Film director	26 December
Jude Law	Actor	29 December

1972 Departures

Maurice Chevalier	Entertainer	(b1888)	1 January
Frederick IX	King of Denmark	(b1899)	14 January
John Grierson	Pioneer documentary-maker	(b1898)	19 February
Walter Winchell	US journalist	(b1897)	20 February
David McCallum Snr	Violinist and father of actor David	(b1897)	21 March
J(oseph) Arthur Rank	Industrialist and film producer	(b1888)	29 March
George Sanders	Actor	(b1906)	25 April
Kwame Nkrumah	Ghanaian politician	(b1909)	27 April
J(ohn) Edgar Hoover	FBI Director	(b1895)	2 May
Dan Blocker	Actor (*Bonanza*)	(b1928)	13 May
Cecil Day Lewis	Poet	(b1904)	22 May
Margaret Rutherford	Actress	(b1892)	22 May
Duke of Windsor	Former King Edward VIII	(b1894)	28 May
Oscar Levant	Pianist and actor	(b1906)	14 August
Francis Chichester	Sailor and aviator	(b1901)	26 August
Prince William of Gloucester		(b1941)	28 August
Leo G. Carroll	Actor	(b1886)	16 October
Igor Sikorsky	Russian aviation pioneer	(b1889)	26 October
Ezra Pound	Poet	(b1885)	1 November
Louella Parsons	Gossip columnist	(b1881)	9 December
Charles Atlas	Strongman and sideshow performer	(b1892)	24 December
Harry S. Truman	Former US President	(b1884)	26 December

Index of operators and vehicles

Buses, Coaches, Trolleybuses, Trams & Recollections 1958

Henry Conn

Contents

© Henry Conn 2016

British Library Cataloguing in Publication Data
A catalogue record for this book is available from the British Library.

Title page: **HEREFORD** In April 1951 Midland Red No 3825 (NHA 825), a Brush-bodied BMMO D5B, entered service from Bearwood depot. In October it was reallocated to Ludlow, and from November 1953 it was based in Hereford. This view was taken at High Town, Hereford, on 30 July 1958, and the bus

Acknowledgments

A large number of the illustrations in this book are from the camera of John Clarke, and without these wonderful views this book would not have been possible. My most sincere thanks to John – outstanding.

Many thanks also to The Transport Treasury for a number of excellent views of the trams in Aberdeen, Glasgow, Blackpool and The Mumbles.

The PSV Circle Fleet Histories for the operators in this book and a number of issues of *Buses Illustrated* were vital sources of information for this book.

ISBN 978 1 85794 464 8

Silver Link Publishing Ltd
The Trundle
Ringstead Road
Great Addington
Kettering
Northants NN14 4BW

Tel/Fax: 01536 330588

email: sales@nostalgiacollection.com
Website: www.nostalgiacollection.com

Printed and bound in the Czech Republic

is working route X34, the 60-mile hourly service between Hereford and Shrewsbury through Ludlow, the longest double-deck route of Midland Red. On the day this view was taken, Kate Bush was born in Bexleyheath. *Author's collection*

About the author

My first recollections of public transport were early in 1958 in my home town of Aberdeen, travelling from our home in Mastrick to Union Street, then onwards by tram to Bridge of Dee. My interest in buses, trolleybuses and trams expanded to taking fleet numbers or registration numbers, and by the mid-1960s I had acquired a camera and began my collection. This interest continued through my family's moves from Aberdeen to Perth, Whitburn in West Lothian, Banbury, Swindon and Oxford by 1974.

My first job was with Customs & Excise, beginning in London with transfers to Oxford, Dover and Brighton. It was after I left Brighton that my enthusiasm for bus photography waned, and it never really returned apart from sporadic photography when I returned to Scotland in 1980. By this time I had left Customs & Excise and had returned to college in Cupar to study Agriculture. I met my future wife at this college and moved with her parents to Galloway, where I have lived very happily since 1983. To further my career I attended Aberdeen University to take a BSc Degree in Agriculture, and I successfully graduated in 1996. This led to me returning to the Civil Service with the Scottish Executive Rural Affairs Department, then through many changes to where I am now, working with Natural England as adviser to farmers on Environmental Schemes (three days a week from last July).

By 2010 I had a significant collection of transport views from the mid-1960s to the early 1980s. I met with Silver Link Publishing's editor Will Adams in Preston in early 2010 and was very kindly given the opportunity to write a volume on Buses, Trams and Trolleybuses in the Midlands. Since then I have continued to enjoy writing volumes on transport for Silver Link, this volume being my fifth in the 'Recollections' series looking at buses, trolleybuses and trams as well as significant events in a specific year.

Introduction

In 1958 the Porsche 718, a mid-engined race car, was introduced to the public and Boris Pasternak was awarded the Nobel Prize for Literature. *Look Back in Anger* with Richard Burton, Claire Bloom and Mary Ure was released, and Paul McCartney invited George Harrison to watch The Quarrymen at the Wilson Hall, opposite Garston bus depot in Liverpool – this was the same day as the Munich air disaster. *South Pacific* was released on 19 March, and seven days later the 30th Academy Awards were broadcast live, and the Best Picture award went to *The Bridge on the River Kwai* and Best Actor was Alec Guinness. On 6 April Arnold Palmer won his first major golf tournament, The Masters. *Gigi*, the musical, was released on 15 May and the following month Nelson Mandela married Winnie Madikizela.

Pizza Hut was founded in the same month in Wichita, Kansas, and on 15 June Brazil beat Sweden 5-2 in Solna, Sweden, to win the World Cup.

A Night to Remember was released on 1 July with Kenneth More leading the cast in a film about the ill-fated *Titanic*. In the same month *The Defiant Ones* with Tony Curtis and Sidney Poitier was released, the story of two convicts who must co-operate to survive. On 15 August Buddy Holly married Marie Elena Santiago and the following day Madonna was born. The controversial novel *Lolita* was published on 18 August and the editor of the London *Sunday Express* called it 'the filthiest book I have ever read' and 'sheer unrestrained pornography'. On the day the film *The Fly* was released, 29 August, Michael Jackson was born and on 20 September *Cat on a Hot Tin Roof* was released, with Elizabeth Taylor, Paul Newman and Burl Ives.

In October *La Bamba*, a folk song recorded by Ritchie Valens, was released; the song charted in early 1959, but on 3 February of that year Ritchie Valens was killed in a plane crash, his recording career having lasted only eight months. On 9 October Pope Pius XII died, and 19 days later John XIII (Angelo Roncalli) was elected Pope. Agatha Christie's book *Ordeal by Innocence* was published on 3 November, and later that month Edward Kennedy married Virginia Joan Bennett. The 1958 Queen's Christmas Broadcast was made live from the Long Library at Sandringham in Norfolk.

In Aberdeen, my home at this time, I vaguely remember the last day of the trams on 3 May. However, I do remember the outrage when all the remaining trams, including the beautiful streamliners featured in this book, were unceremoniously burned by the scrap dealers at Queens links on 12 May.

Enjoy the nostalgia!

Scotland

FORT WILLIAM Waiting at the Grand Hotel in Fort William for passengers for the trip to Inverness on 25 April is Highland Omnibuses' K89 (EST 393), a Strachan-bodied Guy Arab III new in May 1951; it would pass to Western SMT for spares only in June 1969. The Grand Hotel stood proud in High Street and Gordon Square for 72 years, but in December 2011 it took contractors less than 48 hours to demolish the four-storey building using heavy plant machinery. *Author's collection*

Born on this day in Dalkeith was Derek William Dick, better known as Fish, singer with Marillion.

Photo	DESTINATIONS
1	**HEREFORD** *(Title page)*
	SCOTLAND
2	**FORT WILLIAM** *(Previous page)*
3	**ABERDEEN**
4	**ABERDEEN**
5	**GLASGOW**
6	**GLASGOW**
7	**GLASGOW**
8	**GLASGOW**
9	**GLASGOW**
10	**GLASGOW**
11	**GLASGOW**
12	**GLASGOW**
13	**GLASGOW**
14	**GOUROCK**
15	**AYRSHIRE**
16	**DUMFRIES**

ABERDEEN This is Aberdeen Corporation car 26, a Pickering/English Electric all-enclosed streamliner that entered service on 28 April 1949; it is seen here on 20 March 1958 on Union Street. In the background is FAV 333, a Roberts-bodied Foden PVSC6 new in July 1949 to Strachans (Deeside Omnibus Service). *Transport Treasury*

On this day the film Dunkirk starring John Mills and Richard Attenborough was released to cinemas in the UK.

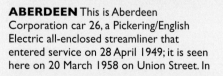

Right: **ABERDEEN** On the same day as the previous view and also in Union Street, this is Aberdeen car 30, which entered service on 10 June 1949; in 1957 all 20 streamliners, Nos 19 to 38, were offered to Glasgow and possibly Blackpool, but could not be sold. These beautiful-looking tramcars, which cost £11,000 each, were sold for scrap for £90 each, and on the night of 12/13 May 1958 were burned on the private track at Queens Links. *Transport Treasury*

Below: **GLASGOW** This is Garelochhead Coach Services' JGD 675, the unique Scottish Aviation-bodied Foden PVD6 new in 1948 and acquired from Foy, Glasgow, in 1951. Scottish Aviation, located at Prestwick Airport in Ayrshire, started out as a flying school but diversified into aircraft maintenance

in 1938 and during the war was responsible for maintaining and modifying Liberator aircraft. During 1947 the company diversified into bus bodywork and the first orders were completed in 1948. The last bus body orders were in 1952, and the company returned to aircraft work and became part of British Aerospace in 1977. This view was taken on 10 June. *Author's collection*

On this day the first parking meters were installed in the UK at Grosvenor Square, near the US Embassy in London; 1 hour cost 6 shillings and the penalty for overstay was £2.

GLASGOW Crossing the tram lines at Saltmarket on 16 October is Central SMT L346 (DVD 204), an all-Leyland PD2/1 new in 1948; it would pass to Western SMT in June 1965 for spares. *Author's collection*

On this day the first ever episode of Blue Peter *was broadcast; almost every episode from 1964 onwards still exists in the BBC archives.*

GLASGOW Working route 29 to Maryhill at Glasgow Cross is Coronation car 1279. The Coronations were first introduced in December 1936 and were considered by many to be Glasgow's finest cars, but there were drawbacks such as a low seating capacity (64) and the running costs. They received several modifications after 1949, one of which was the replacement of the two-piece windscreen with a single panel, as seen in this view taken on 1 August. *Transport Treasury*

The UK No 1 single on this day was the Everly Brothers' All I Have To Do Is Dream.

GLASGOW Tramcar route 18 linked Springburn with Rutherglen by a circuitous route, and the cars were always busy with intermediate traffic rather than over the whole route. The 18 ran beyond the city boundary but was not pruned in 1956/57 and survived with the associated 18A until 3 June 1961. The route passed beneath the aqueduct of the Forth & Clyde Canal, as seen in this view of Coronation car No 1213 on 17 August. *Transport Treasury*

Born on this day in Hollywood, Los Angeles, was singer Belinda Carlisle.

GLASGOW
Coronation cars Nos 1393 to 1398 had bogies and motors from 'Green Goddess' cars purchased from Liverpool, and entered service in 1954; the cars were slightly simpler and neater in design than earlier Coronations. With Bellahouston Park in the background, Coronation 1394 is on Mosspark Boulevard on 2 August 1958. *Transport Treasury*

The No 1 album in the UK was the music from the original cast of My Fair Lady.

GLASGOW En route to Springburn on 24 June at Charing Cross is Coronation car 1275, new in 1940. The bus heading for Knightswood is No AR 301 (BGA 6); originally bodied by Cowieson, this AEC Regent was new in September 1937. Cowieson began building bus bodywork in 1919, and by 1930 the company had become Scotland's leading bus-builder; most Glasgow double-deck buses in the 1930s had Cowieson bodywork. However, by 1938 a contract for double-deck bodywork for Glasgow was re-allocated to MCW when Cowieson was unable to meet the delivery date. The last Cowieson bodies were built in 1939 and the company did not return to bus bodywork after the war. AR 301 received an Alexander body in August 1950 and was sold to Reliance of Newbury in March 1959, where it was used for spares to keep similar bus AR 304 (BGA 9) in service. *John Clarke*

Right: **GLASGOW**
On 25 June, heading through Shawlands for the University, is Standard hex-dash car No 63. The University terminus was served by routes 3 and 14, and a very impressive frequency was maintained, especially in the morning rush to get to lectures at 9.00am. The trams were diverted away from the University terminus in January 1959, and never returned. *John Clarke*

Left: **GLASGOW** Originally built in 1926 as an experimental high-speed car, No 1089 was converted from the original separate entrance and exit to normal layout in 1932, and from that time worked on route 20 between Clydebank and Duntocher until 4 December 1949, when that route closed. A couple of years later, 1089 emerged to work shipyard specials from Partick depot; this view was taken on a miserable 27 June at Partick depot, with Dumbarton Road in the background. *John Clarke*

Left: **GOUROCK** In August 1943 No G78 (GLL 578), a Park Royal-bodied Guy Arab II, entered service with London Transport from Alperton depot. During late November 1951 Western SMT acquired the bus and a further 21 of the same type, eight of which had Park Royal bodywork, four had Massey bodywork and the remaining ten had bodywork by Weymann. G78 was given Western SMT fleet number 997 and received a new Alexander body in 1953. This view of the bus was taken in Gourock on 11 July. *Author's collection*

On this day Peter Manuel was hanged in Barlinnie Prison after being found guilty of a number of murders. He was the third last criminal to be hanged in Scotland; the last hanging took place in Aberdeen in August 1963.

Right: **GLASGOW** Leaving Partick depot on 27 June is Kilmarnock bogie No 1100, which was built by Hurst Nelson in 1928 and externally modified in 1941, giving it some resemblance to the Coronation cars. It also received new stairs and brown leather seats and gave years of service on shipyard specials from Partick depot. *John Clarke*

At the end of March 1958 Sir William Burrell, Glasgow ship owner and art collector, died and bequeathed the Burrell Collection to Glasgow; it eventually opened to the public in 1983 in Pollok Country Park.

Below: **AYRSHIRE** This is RN 8982, an all-Leyland TD7 new in 1940 and purchased by A1 Service of Ardrossan, Ayrshire, in December 1955. On 12 September 1958 the washing hangs out in the court behind the bus, the road is dry, and yet in the distance a lady appears with an umbrella! *Author's collection*

On the day this view was taken, Jack Kilby invented the first integrated circuit.

Above: **DUMFRIES** During 1947 East Yorkshire Motor Services received five new Weymann-bodied Leyland PS1s, Nos 428 to 432 (HAT 644 to 648). In February 1958 they were all withdrawn and sold to Passenger Vehicle Disposals of Leeds, then in June of that year Carruthers of New Abbey acquired HAT 647, and this view was taken in Dumfries on 29 August. The bus in the background is SMT No 454 (JSF 154), an Alexander coach-bodied AEC Regal IV new in 1952, which is working on the Dumfries to Edinburgh service. *Author's collection*

On this day Michael Jackson was born in Gary, Indiana.

FLEETWOOD's Pharos Lighthouse (also known as the Upper Lighthouse) is a 93-foot-tall sandstone lighthouse that was designed in 1839 by Decimus Burton and Capt H. M. Denham. Unusually for a functioning lighthouse, it stands in the middle of a residential street, Pharos Street. The lighthouse was designed and constructed in conjunction with the much shorter 34-foot Lower Lighthouse, which stands on Fleetwood seafront. The lighthouses were designed to be used as a pair to guide shipping through the treacherous sandbanks of the Wyre estuary – the light from the Pharos should be kept immediately above the light from the Lower lighthouse to ensure a safe passage down the channel. Both lighthouses were first illuminated on 1 December 1840, and for many years the Pharos was painted in striking cream and red, as seen in this view.

The Fleetwood terminal loop of the Blackpool tramway runs past the foot of the lighthouse, and in service on Pharos Street on 21 December 1958 is car 255, an EEC 'Balloon' car new in December 1934. *Transport Treasury*

On this day Charles de Gaulle was elected President of France with 78.5% of the votes.

BLACKPOOL At midday on a rainy 22 December, with Blackpool Tower in the background, we see EEC 'Balloon' No 250, which was new in December 1934. *Transport Treasury*

The No 1 single for the 1958 festive period was Conway Twitty's It's Only Make Believe.

Below: **BLACKPOOL** From July 1928 to January 1929 Blackpool took delivery of ten 'Pantograph' cars, Nos 167 to 176. They were purchased to improve operations on the North Station to Fleetwood section, and this is No 175 at North Station on 5 July 1958. This tram was withdrawn in 1960 and scrapped at Marton depot in early 1963. It is likely that the film on at the Odeon is the excellent *Ice Cold in Alex* with John Mills and Anthony Quayle. *John Clarke*

Above: **BLACKPOOL** Between July and October 1937 Blackpool Corporation took delivery of its last Brush-bodied cars, Nos 284 to 303, and representing this batch on 20 October is No 292, which was re-numbered 629 in May 1968, withdrawn from service in November 1972, and scrapped at Blundell Street Depot in early 1980. *Transport Treasury*

In New York on this day Viggo Mortensen was born, perhaps best known for his role as Aragorn in the 'Lord of the Rings' films.

1958
No 1 Records

January
| Jerry Lee Lewis | *Great Balls of Fire* |
| Elvis Presley | *Jailhouse Rock* |

February
| Michael Holliday | *The Story of my Life* |
| Perry Como | *Magic Moments* |

April
| Marvin Rainwater | *Whole Lotta Woman* |

May
| Connie Francis | *Who's Sorry Now?* |

June
| Vic Damone | *On the Street Where You Live* |

July
| Everly Brothers | *All I Have to do is Dream/Claudette* |

August
| Kalin Twins | *When* |

September
| Connie Francis | *Carolina Moon/Stupid Cupid* |

November
| Tommy Edwards | *It's All in the Game* |
| Lord Rockingham's XI | *Hoots Mon* |

December
| Conway Twitty | *It's Only Make Believe* |

BLACKPOOL During 1935 20 Series 2 Railcoaches entered service, Nos 264 to 283. No 276 was withdrawn in February 1957 and 275 in early 1958 for rebuilding; in April 1958 276 entered experimental service with 275 as its trailer, and this view of the pair was taken at Central Station on 5 July. *John Clarke*

Below: **ACCRINGTON** Infant Street, Accrington, behind Accrington Corporation's No 2 (JTF 738), was home to a branch of Whitewell Dairies Ltd of Stanley Street, Accrington, which specialised in ice creams. The gable-end advert is for Lanry, a locally produced bleach. No 2, seen here on 27 September 1958, was a Burlingham-bodied Leyland PS1 new in 1948, and sold for scrap in 1965. *Author's collection*

On the day this view was taken Hurricane Helene, the worst storm of the Atlantic hurricane season, reached category 4 status, the second-highest classification, with sustained winds of 135mph.

Above: **MORECAMBE** En route to Heysham Village on Marine Road, Morecambe, at its junction with Clarence Road on 7 August is Morecambe & Heysham No 58 (KTF 587), a Park Royal-bodied AEC Regent III new in August 1949; it was later converted to open-top form in 1970. The carriage driver is looking for custom along the seafront. *Author's collection*

On this day Bruce Dickinson, vocalist with Samson and Iron Maiden, was born in Worksop.

Manchester and Liverpool

MANCHESTER A total of 45 Crossley 'Empire' TDD 42s were built between 1950 and 1951, 38 of which went new to Manchester, five were supplied to Ashton, and Cleethorpes purchased two. Working a 'Special' on 15 July 1958 is No 1210 (JVU 717); together with all the other Crossley 'Empires' it was sold for scrap in 1963. *Author's collection*

On this day Julia Lennon, mother of John Lennon, was struck and killed by a car in Liverpool.

MANCHESTER In a rather precarious position in Piccadilly Gardens on 7 June, working service 218 to Stalybridge, is Ashton-under-Lyne Corporation No 89 (YTE 828), a Bond-bodied BUT 9612T new in October 1956; it was withdrawn after a working life of ten years in October 1966. In the background is Lewis's store; the first Lewis's was opened in 1856 in Liverpool by entrepreneur David Lewis. The first store outside Liverpool opened in nearby Manchester in 1877, and included a full-scale ballroom on the fifth floor, which was also used for exhibitions. *Author's collection*

On this day in Minneapolis, Prince was born.

MANCHESTER The first AEC Regent Vs for A. Mayne & Sons were UNF 10 to 12, bodied by Park Royal and delivered in July 1957. Operating the service to Kershaw Lane, Audenshaw, and turning into Great Ancoats Street on 24 January is a very clean and smart-looking UNF 12; this bus and UNF 11 were withdrawn in 1974 but saw further service with Wards of Epping, while UNF 10 remained with Mayne until 1977. Note the strange place to stand for the gentleman with the newspapers! *Author's collection*

On this day the pianist and television presenter Jools Holland was born in Blackheath, London.

MANCHESTER During 1953 six Leyland PSU1/13s, Nos 30 to 35 (NNB 130 to 135), were delivered for airport work, with raised-roof bodywork. The first three (Nos 30 to 32) carried bodywork by Bond on Burlingham frames, whilst the others carried Burlingham bodywork, all in a livery of two shades of blue with a silver band at windscreen level. This is No 33 (NNB 133), photographed on 10 September; it passed to Young of Maghera, Northern Ireland, in 1968 and was noted with a contractor in Ballymena in September of that year. *Author's collection*

On this day Siobhan Fahey of Bananarama and Shakespear's Sister was born in Dublin.

MANCHESTER Standing in Piccadilly on the same day is No 32 (NNB 132), one of the batch with Bond bodywork on Burlingham frames. Behind it is No 3324 (NNB 164), an NCME-bodied Leyland PD2 12 new in 1953. No 32 was withdrawn in 1967 and passed to Davies of Tredegar, remaining there until October 1968, while 3324 passed to SELNEC on 1 November 1969, as a withdrawn-from-service bus. *Author's collection*

Right: **MANCHESTER** Six Manchester Corporation buses stand outside the six-storey Ducie Street Goods Depot. Nearest the camera is No 2044 (GVR 138), an all-Crossley DD42/4 new in 1948; next in line is sister vehicle No 2033, new in 1947; the DD42/4 was 8 feet wide and had a Crossley HOE 7/1 8.6-litre direct-injection engine. No 2033 remained in the fleet until 1963, and 2044 was sold in 1966. *Author's collection*

Below: **MANCHESTER** The New Inn used to stand on the corner of Moston Lane and Rochdale Road in Harpurhey, east Manchester. It was built in about 1829 and by the 1870s was owned by Chesters Brewery. It later passed to Threlfalls, then Whitbread in 1967 before being bricked up and demolished in 1978. Exiting Moston Lane on 20 October is No 3040 (GVR 242), an MCCW-bodied Leyland PD1 new in 1947 and sold for scrap in 1963. *Author's collection*

On this day Mark King of Level 42 was born in Cowes on the Isle of Wight.

Right: **MANCHESTER** On 12 July, working route 117, is Manchester Corporation No 4083 (GVR 385), a Brush-bodied Daimler CVG5 new in 1948; it was sold for scrap 20 years later. *Author's collection*

On this day the Beatles, then known as the Quarrymen, paid 17s 6d to have their first recording session, where they recorded Buddy Holly's That'll be the Day and In Spite of all the Danger, a song written by Paul McCartney and George Harrison.

MANCHESTER This is Manchester Corporation No 3278 (JND 679), an all-Leyland PD2/3 working route 62 from Heaton Park to Chorlton (Ryebank Road) on 5 March. A batch of 100 buses, Manchester's first PD2s, was delivered in 1950/51, with four entering service in 1952. Nos 3200 to 3264 had Metro-Cammell bodies of the standard post-war Manchester design, while Nos 3265 to 3299, which were delivered first, had the flush-mounted windows of the standard

Leyland Farington body; No 3278 was withdrawn in 1969. The three gentlemen on the right don't seem to have a care in the world! *Author's collection*

5 March 1958 was the birthday of Andy Gibb, the youngest of the Brothers Gibb, best known as the Bee Gees.

Right: **MANCHESTER** Standing in Piccadilly on 6 February is No 4407 (NNB 217), an MCCW-bodied Daimler CVG6K new in 1953. This was a sad day for the public of Manchester as news filtered through that seven Manchester United footballers were among the 21 people who lost their lives in the Munich air disaster; 23 people survived but unfortunately, 15 days after the crash, Duncan Edwards, at the tender age of 21, died from his injuries. *Author's collection*

Below: **MANCHESTER** Twenty MCCW Orion-bodied Daimlers were delivered to Manchester in 1955, 19 of which were CVG5Ks; the other, No 4490 (PND 490), was a CLG5K, the CL being the lightweight version of the CV, saving around 10cwt. By 1955 all the weight-saving features were available or incorporated into the CV, so No 4490, photographed here on 30 August, was one of the last CLs to be produced. *Author's collection*

Later this day, and for a number of nights afterwards, the Notting Hill race riots took place.

Above: **MANCHESTER** The 90 Daimlers delivered between 1954 and 1955 were the first Manchester buses with concealed radiators, as seen here on 5 December with Daimler CVG6K No 4483 (NNB 293); note the partial covering of the radiator grill for heat retention. *Author's collection*

On this day Prime Minister Harold Macmillan opened the Preston bypass, the UK's first stretch of motorway.

Above right: **MANCHESTER** Corporation was keen to get the maximum number of passengers on its MCCW-bodied Leyland PD2/40s, and specified this very upright style of bodywork, which was unique to the city. Working service 19 to West Didsbury on 10 September is No 3544 (UNB 544), which was new in 1958. *Author's collection*

Born on this day was Chris Columbus, the film director best known for Mrs Doubtfire, Home Alone *and two of the 'Harry Potter' movies.*

Opposite page: **MANCHESTER** Standing amidst a plethora of gable-end advertising on 20 September is No 3953 (GNA 162), which was new in 1940 as No 953 and was subsequently re-numbered in 1946; it is a Leyland TD5 with a Crossley body and MCCW frames, and was one of the last TD5s to be withdrawn from the Manchester Corporation fleet in 1962. Did you know that Mackintosh's Rolo was first sold in 1937, and that Rowntree's KitKat, originally called 'Rowntree's Chocolate Crisp', first went on sale in 1935 and changed its name to KitKat after the Second World War. Older still, Senior Service cigarettes, with the logo of the sailing ship, were officially launched in 1925. *Author's collection*

MANCHESTER Seen in Parker Street are North Western Road Car Nos 231 (left) and 226 (CDB 231 and CDB 226), both all-Leyland PD2/1s new in 1948. In the background is the dome of the Rylands Building, which is now Grade II listed; it was originally built as a warehouse by the Rylands textile company and was designed by Manchester architect Fairhursts. Following a fire in 1957, which destroyed the premises of Paulden's Department Store, the company acquired the Rylands warehouse building and converted it to a store. In 1973 Paulden's was rebranded Debenhams, and the building has carried that name ever since. This view was taken on 20 April. *Author's collection*

MANCHESTER A total of 40 Bristol L5Gs were delivered to North Western during 1946 and early 1947; Nos 101 to 135 had Brush bodywork and 136 to 140 had bodywork by ECW. Many of the batch were rebodied between 1956 and 1958 with 1948 Weymann bodies from pre-war Bristols. One of these, originally numbered 103, and seen here on 18 May 1958 after rebodying, was renumbered 98 (BJA 403). In the background is the back end of No 33 (NNB 133), one of the Burlingham-bodied Leyland PSU1/13 Manchester Corporation airline buses. *Author's collection*

On this day an F104 Starfighter set a world speed record of 1,404.19mph.

SALFORD During the autumn of 1948 Salford Corporation took delivery of eight MCCW-bodied Daimler CVD6s, Nos 343 to 350 (CRJ 343 to 350); they were a diverted order, surplus to the requirements of Chester Corporation. In 1948 a new General Manager changed Salford's livery to green and cream and the title of the undertaking to Salford City Transport. Also, the radiator badges fixed by the manufacturers were removed and replaced by a badge enamelled in green and cream, bearing the title of the undertaking. No 344 (CRJ 344) is seen here on 3 January. *Author's collection*

Two days before this view the European Economic Community (EEC) was founded, and the first formal meeting was held on 16 January.

SOUTH MANCHESTER

A total of 40 ECW-bodied Bristol K5Gs entered service with North Western in 1939, registered AJA 144 to 183); all were re-bodied by Willowbrook during 1951 and 1952. This is No 463 (AJA 183), the last of the batch of 40, off duty on 15 May; it would be one of the last to survive in the North Western fleet, being sold for scrap in 1965. *Author's collection*

Gigi opened on this day in New York City after being shown at the Cannes Film Festival; the last of the great MGM musicals, it went on to win nine Academy Awards, including Best Picture.

STOCKPORT During 1953 North Western Road Car took delivery of Nos 514 to 549 (FDB 514 to 549), all Weymann-bodied Leyland PSU1/13s, and representing this batch is No 518 (FDB 518), seen in Stockport on 5 December. In the background is No 552 (FDB 552), a side-gangway Weymann-bodied Leyland PD2/12. No 518 passed to Lynch of Passage East, Ireland, in January 1967 and remained with that operator until 1971. *Author's collection*

On this day the Queen inaugurated STD (Subscriber Trunk Dialling) with a call from Bristol to Edinburgh.

DIDSBURY There were two routes from Stockport to Altrincham, the 71 via Cheadle and the 80 via Heaton Mersey and Didsbury. Working the 80 at Didsbury on 29 July is North Western No 260, a Weymann-bodied Leyland PD2/1 new in 1949; it was withdrawn in 1966, noted with C&W of Bishopbriggs in February 1968, and had been scrapped by that October. *Author's collection*

On this day the US Congress formally created the National Aeronautics and Space Administration (NASA).

Right: **LIVERPOOL** Standing on Mann Island on 30 May is Liverpool Corporation No L113 (RKC 214), a very smart Duple-bodied Leyland PD2/20 new in March 1955. *Author's collection*

Born on this day in Sweden was singer Gun-Marie Fredriksson. Who? The Top 10 hits Listen to Your Heart *and* It Must Have Been Love *are clues to the lead vocalist of Scandinavia's most successful act in the USA at the time … Roxette.*

Below: **ST HELENS** On route 7 on 9 April is St Helens Corporation No 376 (BDJ 76), an East Lancashire-bodied Sunbeam F4 new in December 1950. In July all eight Sunbeam F4s (BDJ 74 to 81) were sold to South Shields Corporation, and No 376 became South Shields 203 and entered service in August 1958, remaining there until its sale for scrap in April 1963. The Crosville ECW-bodied Bristol LD in the background is heading for Speke. *John Clarke*

Leeds and Sheffield

LEEDS Car No 509 is seen in the tranquil setting of Temple Newsam on Friday 20 June, but in a short space of time this scene would be all but a memory. The run to Temple Newsam was a pleasant journey through the woods and cars would often reach high speeds as they ran downhill towards the city. The service was always busy during the summer months, but during winter the half-hourly service often ran empty. *John Clarke*

Three weeks later appearing at the Leeds Empire were Shirley Bassey, billed as 'Britain's sepia songstress', and Des O'Connor, billed as 'Comedy in the Modern Manner'.

January
> The European Economic Community is founded
> Sputnik 1, launched in October 1957, falls to Earth
> The first successful US satellite, Explorer 1, is launched into orbit.

February
> Egypt and Syria unite to form the United Arab Republic, and Gamal Nasser becomes first President
> A hydrogen bomb is lost in the waters off Georgia, USA
> Seven Manchester United footballers are among 21 people killed in Munich air disaster
> Pope Pius XII declares St Clare the patron saint of television
> Bertrand Russell launches the Campaign for Nuclear Disarmament

March
> British and Commonwealth team led by Sir Vivian Fuchs completes first overland crossing of Antarctic, using snowcat caterpillar tractors and dogsled teams
> The US Army launches Explorer 3
> *The Bridge on the River Kwai* wins seven awards at the 30th Academy Awards
> Nikita Khrushchev becomes Premier of the Soviet Union

April
> BBC Radiophonic Workshop is established
> In Cuba, Castro's revolutionary army begins attacks on Havana

LEEDS An Art Moderne-style cinema situated at the junction of Roundhay Road and Easterly Road, the Clock was built for West Leeds Entertainments and opened on 21 November 1938 with *The Hurricane* starring Dorothy Lamour. The name of the cinema was taken from the name of the building it occupied, the Clock Building, which has a clock made by William Potts & Sons of Leeds. The cinema was designed by Norman Fowler of Messrs Kitson, Parish, Ledgard & Pyman of Leeds, and built by C. H. F. Lax & Co. As well as the large auditorium, with 1,130 stalls seats and 706 in the balcony, there was a spacious foyer, a café, a parade of shops and a car park for 200 vehicles. The cinema closed on 28 February 1976 with the featured film *The Incredible Journey*, and became a bingo hall, which in turn subsequently closed and the Clock was gutted and transformed into a large electrical goods retailer on the ground floor and offices on two levels above. Passing the Clock on 20 June is Horsfield car No 229, which was sold to George Cohen for scrap in June 1959. *John Clarke*

LEEDS This lovely view shows workmen on the tram line at Gledhow Wood Road on 20 June, with Horsfield car No 196 about to pass them. No 196 would remain in the tram fleet until sold for scrap in June 1959. The lorry on the right is a Bedford, and the partially visible car is a Hillman. *John Clarke*

1958 Happenings (2)

April *continued*
   First CND protest march from Hyde Park to
      Aldermaston
   Satellite Sputnik 2 disintegrates in space after
      several orbits
   King of Belgium opens World's Fair, Expo 58, in
      Brussels

May
   Actor-singer Paul Robeson sells out two one-
      man concerts at Carnegie Hall, but is seldom
      seen in public in the US again
   Military coup in Algeria
   Soviet Union launches Sputnik 3
   Cuban government launches counter-offensive
      against Castro's rebels
   Real Madrid win European Cup

June
   Charles de Gaulle is brought out of retirement
      to lead France by decree for six months
   Pizza Hut is founded
   World's last fully rigged sailing ship trading under
      sail alone, built in 1887, sinks
   Brazil wins football World Cup

July
   Earthquake in Alaska causes landslide and mega-
      tsunami, with waves reaching 525m (1,722ft)
   First parking meters installed in UK
   Revolution in Iraq – King Faisal killed, and Abdul
      Qassim assumes power
   5,000 US Marines land in Beirut, Lebanon, to
      protect pro-Western government there
   First life peerage created in UK
   US launches Explorer 4

LEEDS In the right background of this view is the creation of watchmaker John Dyson in 1876, although behind the elaborate frontage are two 17th-century houses. The gilded time ball mechanism was linked to Greenwich and dropped at exactly 1pm each day; this feature, together with the window mechanism, makes Dyson's a rare survivor of elaborate Victorian/Edwardian shop innovation and design. A Grade II listed building, the ground floor is now an Indian restaurant, but it was still Dyson's until the late 1990s. Passing the building on 20 June 1958 is Feltham car No 582, which was sold for scrap in August of the following year. *John Clarke*

LEEDS It is late afternoon on 20 July in Bridge End, and the cyclist, I am sure, is heading for home, being chased by Feltham No 529 heading for Crossgates; this tram would remain in the fleet until the end of tramway operations, and was scrapped by J. W. Hinchcliffe at Swinegate depot in February 1960. *John Clarke*

The film at the movies in Leeds in July 1958 would have been A Night to Remember *with Kenneth More, an account of the ill-fated maiden voyage of RMS* Titanic *in 1912.*

SHEFFIELD During the Second World War Sheffield Corporation purchased 10 trams from Bradford and 14 from Newcastle Corporation. One of the Bradford cars, No 330, had its top deck removed and became a rail grinder in the works fleet, surviving as such until the end of the tramway operations in the city. No 330 is seen here exiting Tenter Street depot on 19 June; this depot was the last operational tram depot and the bus depot, on the upper level, was accessed from Hawley Street. *John Clarke*

Appearing at Sheffield City Hall on 11 June were The Treniers, Chas McDevitt Skiffle Group, the Hedley Ward Trio, and Terry Wayne.

SHEFFIELD With one man captured floating across the pedestrian crossing, the jackets and coats that all are wearing in this view do not suggest that it is the height of summer, yet the date is 19 June and approaching the camera is Sheffield Standard car No 170. During this week in the city the weather became unseasonably cool at times, and on the 19th the temperature only reached 12°C. *John Clarke*

The Midlands

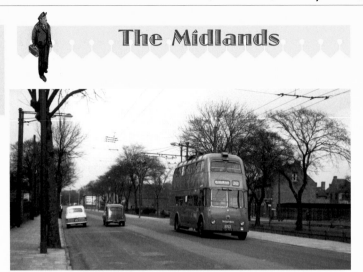

passed to West Midlands Passenger Transport Executive on 1 October 1969, and No 198 survived until it was sold for scrap in March 1976. *Author's collection*

On this day Iceland extended its fishing limits to 12 miles, and three months later the first 'Cod War' with the UK began.

Left: **BLOXWICH** Walsall's Nos 851 to 865 were the first double-deck vehicles on two-axle chassis in the country with an overall length of 30 feet. All were Sunbeam F4As bodied by Willowbrook, and new in January 1955 was No 852, seen here in Bloxwich on 16 April; all would pass to the West Midlands PTE on 1 October 1969, and all had been withdrawn by October 1970. *John Clarke*

The following day the World's Fair in Brussels opened, also known as Expo 58.

Left: **WALSALL** acquired two Roe-bodied Karrier W4s (FTG 697 and 698) from Pontypridd Urban District Council in December 1955, and allocated them the fleet numbers 301 and 302; this is No 302 in Wisemore, Walsall, on 16 April. It remained in the fleet until sold for scrap in April 1963. *John Clarke*

Left: **WEST BROMWICH** Corporation took delivery of 12 Willowbrook-bodied Daimler CVG6s in January 1957. Representing this batch on 1 June is No 198 (PEA 198), working route 14 to West Bromwich. All 12 buses

At the time this photograph was taken you might be singing along to Perry Como's Magic Moments *and* Catch a Falling Star.

Swansea & Mumbles

MUMBLES The Swansea to Mumbles Pier line was electrified in 1928, with trials beginning in July of that year. A fleet of 11 double-deck cars were built by Brush Electrical Company of Loughborough and full electrical services were started with these cars on 2 March 1929. These cars were the largest ever built for service in Britain and each could seat 106 passengers; they were also frequently operated in pairs, giving a total capacity of 212. Two further cars were added later, bringing the fleet strength up to 13. Mumbles Pier, in the background, is 835 feet long and was built in 1898 at a cost of around £10,000. Leaving the pier terminus on 8 July is car 9 with car 11 attached. *Transport Treasury*

On this day actor Kevin Bacon was born in Philadelphia – who remembers the film Footloose?

MUMBLES It is clear from this view of the same two cars taken on the same day that two cars were often operated in pairs. In 1958 the South Wales Transport Company, the principal operator of motor bus services in the Swansea town area, purchased the railway, and it was closed in two stages, with the section from Southend to the Pier closing on 11 October 1959 for construction of a road to the Pier for the buses that were to replace the trams; the last car operated on Tuesday 5 January 1960. *Transport Treasury*

Hammersmith Road between Blythe Road and Brook Green became one vast manufacturing complex with more than 30,000 staff working there. The vehicles employed were mostly normal-control Morris Commercials, with a few forward-control Thornycrofts from the Nippy or Sturdy ranges, having the 1949/50-style cab shared with contemporary Guy models. The latter were not liked by the regular drivers because of poor acceleration, an awkward gear-change and a climb into the cab compared with the step-in Morris Commercials. *John Clarke*

London

Born on this day was American actress Rachel Ticotin, whose films include Con-Air *and* Total Recall.

MOORGATE was an important city terminus for London trolleybuses, used by six routes, the 641 from Winchmore Hill being the most frequent; car No 881 is seen at the junction of East Road and City Road on 1 November.

Lyons was run from its vast headquarters, Cadby Hall, at 66 Hammersmith Road, Olympia, west London. At the peak of the company's operations, the entire stretch of land along the

HIGHBURY
This is Canonbury Road before the one-way system in mid-afternoon on 31 March, and working the 611 route to Highgate Village is L1 No 1359; travelling away in the opposite direction is J3 No 1039. *John Clarke*

Just six days earlier Buddy Holly and the Crickets were in concert at the Gaumont in Hammersmith, and That'll be the Day, Peggy Sue and Oh Boy had all been released as singles before the event.

1958
Happenings (3)

July *continued*
Queen Elizabeth II gives Prince Charles the title Prince of Wales
National Aeronautics and Space Administration (NASA) established

August
Last *Tom and Jerry* cartoon made by Hanna-Barbera – characters not seen again until 1961
Nuclear-powered submarine USS *Nautilus* is first vessel to cross North Pole under water
Nabokov's controversial novel Lolita published in USA
Civil war in China
US begins nuclear tests over South Atlantic
Notting Hill race riots

September
First 'Cod War' begins between UK and Iceland
Majority in France vote yes to constitution of the Fifth Republic

October
Guinea declares itself independent from France
BOAC becomes first airline to fly jet passenger services across the Atlantic, using De Havilland Comets
Pioneer 1 is first spacecraft launched by newly formed NASA

ISLINGTON At the junction of Canal Bridge and a very quiet New North Road on 1 November is No 756 on route 641. *John Clarke*

The No 1 single on this day was Connie Francis with Stupid Cupid.

Right: **ISLINGTON** Exiting Upper Street on 31 March is J2 No 924. Alongside the trolleybus, working service 30 between Roehampton and Hackney Wick, is RTL 1624 (OLD 853), a Weymann-bodied Leyland 7RT that was new in October 1954. *John Clarke*

Far left: **STRATFORD BROADWAY** is dominated by the Anglican Parish Church, which was built between 1832 and 1834 by Edward Blore using grey brick. The most notable feature is a three-stage tower, surmounted by a spire supported with flying buttresses; it is a Grade II listed building. Nearest the camera on the 699 route to Victoria and Albert Docks is No 602C, and on the 669 route to North Woolwich is No 593; this view was taken just before midday on 23 July. *John Clarke*

Right: **ILFORD** depot was the home of the 43 trolleybuses destined for South Africa but diverted to London Transport. They were 8 feet wide and received special dispensation from the Ministry of Transport to operate out of Ilford. They were classified SA, and could only initially operate on routes 691 and 693. Working the 693 to Chadwell Heath at Ilford Town Hall on 23 July is No 1750; on the left No 1606 working route 663 is heading for Aldgate, the busiest central London trolleybus terminus. *John Clarke*

Above: **ILFORD** The 695 between Bow and Chadwell Heath was London's newest trolleybus route, starting on 29 October 1941. This view of No 1576 on Ilford High Road was taken on 23 July; six months later route 695 was withdrawn. Behind 1576 is RT 312 (HLX 129), which entered service from Turnham Green depot with a Park Royal roof-box body in February 1948; after overhaul at Aldenham, it was transferred to Forest Gate depot and is seen here working route 25 to Victoria. *John Clarke*

Right: **HAMMERSMITH** The 660 route ran between Hammersmith Broadway and North Finchley, and working the route at the junction of Studland Street and Glenthorne Road on 22 October is No 314. *John Clarke*

Four days later the first transatlantic flight of a Pan American Boeing 707 took place between New York and Paris.

Southern England

Right: **BRIGHTON** The Seven Dials district sits perched on a hilltop north-west of the city centre and is an area of mainly mid-to-late-19th-century architecture. Its name derives from the seven roads that meet at the Seven Dials roundabout; clockwise from the north, they are Prestonville Road, Chatham Place (leading to New England Road and Preston Circus), Buckingham Place (leading to Brighton railway station), Dyke Road, which is a main road in Brighton and Hove leading to Brighton city centre, Vernon Terrace (leading to Montpelier Road and the seafront), Goldsmid Road (leading to Hove), and the northward continuation of Dyke Road leading to Devil's Dyke on the South Downs. At Seven Dials on 30 August is Brighton, Hove & District No 341 (CPM 62), a Weymann-bodied AEC 661T delivered in 1939, stored during the war, and put into service in January 1945. *John Clarke*

The No 1 single on this day was the Kalin Twins with When.

Left: **BRIGHTON** This is Brighton, Hove & District No 294 (DNJ 994), one of three Weymann-bodied BUT 9611Ts that entered service in March 1948. They were used primarily on Brighton systems 41 and 42, Queens Park Circular services, and the 43, 43A and 44 services to Race Hill and Black Rock, operating out of Whitehawk depot. No 294 is seen here operating service 44 in Roedean Road on 25 August 1958. They were the company's only post-war trolleybuses and were sold to Bournemouth in early March 1959. *John Clarke*

Film director Tim Burton was born in Burbank, California, on this day.

Below: **BRIGHTON** Exiting St James's Street into Old Steine at 2.15pm, also on 30 August, is Brighton Corporation No 34 (FUF 34), a Weymann-bodied AEC 661T new in 1939 and sold for scrap in July 1961. In 1958 the Astoria in Brighton was renovated, and the changes, which cost £20,000 (£420,000 at today's values) and reduced the capacity to 1,200, were completed during the summer. On 2 August the Astoria reopened with a five-month run of *South Pacific* – no film had ever had such a long run in Brighton. *John Clarke*

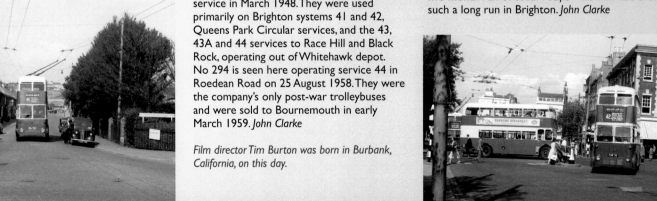

Top left: **BRIGHTON** This is the Aquarium (the Old Steine terminus) on the same day. It had three lines going clockwise round the island: the 26 and 26A took the inner line, 46 and 46A the middle line, and 41, 42, 43A and 48 the outer line. On the 26A is No 44 (FUF 44), on the 46A is No 49 (HUF 49), and on the 41 is No 32 (FUF 32); 32 and 44 are Weymann-bodied AEC 661Ts new in 1939, and 49 is a Weymann-bodied BUT 9611T new in 1948, which was bought by Bradford in February 1959 and sold for scrap in May 1965. *John Clarke*

Centre left: **BRIGHTON** On the same day again, with Brighton Racecourse in the background, this is Brighton, Hove & District No 347 (CPM 997), a Weymann-bodied AEC 661T that was delivered in 1939 and, after storage, entered service in May 1946; it was withdrawn in 1959. *John Clarke*

Below: **BRIGHTON** In the late afternoon of 30 August at Carden Hill is Brighton Corporation No 52 (LCD 52), a Weymann-built BUT 9611T that entered service on 25 March 1953, and was withdrawn and sold to Maidstone Corporation in February 1959. In April 1967 it was withdrawn again and sold for preservation. *John Clarke*

1958 Happenings (4)

October (continued)
Blue Peter is first broadcast
Life Peerages Act entitles women to sit in House of Lords
Boris Pasternak wins Nobel Prize for Literature
First transatlantic flight of a Pan-Am Boeing 707
Pope John XXIII appointed Pope following death of Pius XII

November
New UNESCO building is inaugurated in Paris
Bossa nova dance introduced in Rio de Janeiro
French Sudan, Chad, Republic of the Congo and Gabon become autonomous republics within French colonial empire

December
Subscriber Trunk Dialling (STD) inaugurated in UK
Preston Bypass, Britain's first stretch of motorway, is opened
US launches SCORE, world's first communications satellite
Charles de Gaulle elected President of France
Rebel troops under Che Guevara invade Santa Clara, Cuba, and President Batista resigns two days later

Left: **BRIGHTON** Leaving the Race Hill terminus for the journey to the Aquarium at 3.10 in the afternoon of 30 August is No 41 (FUF 41), a Weymann-bodied AEC 661T new in 1939 and sold for scrap an the end of the Brighton system in June 1961. *John Clarke*

Centre left: **MAIDSTONE** Working service 11 at St Helens on 26 August is Maidstone & District No 16 (BDY 791), a Park Royal-bodied AEC 661T new in June 1940 and scrapped in February 1959. *John Clarke*

A few hours before this photograph was taken, the composer Ralph Vaughan Williams died at 10 Hanover Terrace, Regent's Park, London.

Bottom left: **CANTERBURY** The Westgate, providing the background to this view, is the 60-foot-high medieval western gate of the city wall, and the largest surviving city gate in England. Built of Kentish ragstone around 1379, it is the last survivor of Canterbury's seven medieval gates. The bus seen here on 29 August is East Kent's EFN 190, a Park Royal-bodied Guy Arab III new in 1950, and sold for scrap in January 1969. *Author's collection*

On this day Kent County Cricket Club was playing its third day against New Zealand at the St Lawrence Ground.

Right: **HASTINGS** The Albert Memorial clock tower was commissioned by Hastings Corporation at a cost of £860, and was designed by Edward Heffer of Liverpool following a competition involving 38 competitors and a 10-guinea prize. The foundation stone was laid on 10 November 1862 and work was completed by December 1863, but the clock and dials were not installed immediately; the clock was made by Thwaites & Reed of Clerkenwell and was installed on 10 June 1864 by John Murray Junior of Castle Street, St Leonards. Sadly, at a Hastings Council meeting in October 1973 the decision was taken to demolish the memorial as soon as possible; demolition began in November and took two weeks.

Heading straight towards the camera of John Clarke on 26 August at 1.30 in the afternoon is Maidstone & District No 23 (BDY 798), a Park Royal-bodied Sunbeam W4 new in February 1946; it was acquired by Bradford Corporation in July 1959 and sold for scrap in April 1964. *John Clarke*

1958 Arrivals & Departures

Arrivals

Jools Holland	Musician	24 January	Benjamin Zephaniah	Writer and musician	15 April	Michael Flatley	Dancer	16 July
Ellen deGeneres	Actress and comedienne	26 January	Andie MacDowell	Actress	21 April	Kate Bush	Musician	30 July
Ice-T (Tracy Morrow)	Rapper, songwriter and actor	16 February	Derek Dick ('Fish')	Singer	25 April	Bruce Dickinson	Musician	7 August
			Michelle Pfeiffer	Actress	29 April	Madonna Ciccone (Madonna)	Singer and actress	16 August
Mary Chapin Carpenter	Singer	21 February	Catherine Tate	Comedienne and actress	12 May	Belinda Carlisle	Singer	17 August
Nik Kershaw	Singer	1 March	Paul Whitehouse	Comedian and actor	17 May	Tim Burton	Film director	25 August
Miranda Richardson	Actress	3 March				Michael Jackson	Singer	29 August
Andy Gibb	Singer	5 March	Toyah Willcox	Singer and actress	18 May	Chris Columbus	Film director	10 September
Rik Mayall	Comedian and actor	7 March	Paul Weller	Singer/songwriter	25 May	Siobhan Fahey	Singer	10 September
			Annette Bening	Actress	29 May	Andrea Bocelli	Tenor	22 September
Gary Numan	Singer	8 March	Prince Rogers Nelson (Prince)	Musician	7 June	Irvine Welsh	Author	27 September
Sharon Stone	Actress	10 March				Tim Robbins	Actor	16 October
Linda Robson	Actress	13 March	Esa-Pekka Salonen	Conductor and composer	30 June	Viggo Mortensen	Actor	20 October
Holly Hunter	Actress	20 March				Simon Le Bon	Singer	27 October
Gary Oldman	Actor	21 March	Jennifer Saunders	Comedienne and actress	6 July	Mary Elizabeth Mastrantonio	Actress	17 November
Alec Baldwin	Actor	3 April	Kevin Bacon	Actor	8 July	Jamie Lee Curtis	Actress	22 November
Peter Capaldi	Actor	14 April	Pauline Quirke	Actress	8 July	Nick Park	Animator	6 December
			Fiona Shaw	Actress	10 July	Alannah Myles	Singer/songwriter	25 December

Departures

Edna Purviance	Actress	(b1895)	11 January	Gladys Presley	Mother of Elvis	(b1912)	14 August
Ernst Heinkel	Aircraft designer and manu-facturer	(b1888)	30 January	Ralph Vaughan Williams	Composer	(b1872)	26 August
Christabel Pankhurst	Suffragette	(b 1880)	13 February	Marie Stopes	Birth control pioneer	(b1880)	2 October
Duncan Edwards	Manchester Utd footballer	(b1936)	21 February	Pius XII	Pope	(b1876)	9 October
Harry Cohn	Film producer	(b1891)	27 February	Tyrone Power	Actor	(b1914)	15 November
Mike Todd	Film producer	(b1909)	22 March				
W. C. Handy	Blues composer	(b1873)	28 March				
Ronald Colman	Actor	(b1891)	19 May				
Robert Donat	Actor	(b1905)	9 June				
Julia Lennon	Mother of John Lennon	(b1914)	15 July				
Harry Warner	Warner Bros studio executive	(b1881)	25 July				

SOUTHAMPTON

To replace its trams, Southampton Corporation purchased new a large fleet of Park Royal-bodied Guy Arab IIs and IIIs, and during March and April 1949 a total of 28 of this mark entered service. Representing them is No 158 (FTR 505), which remained in the fleet until it was sold in February 1967. Between 1919 and 1958 flying boats operated a passenger and mail service from Southampton; BOAC ceased its flying boat operations in 1950, but Aquila Airways continued the service until 1958. *Author's collection*

Front cover: **DUBLIN** The Hill of Howth tramway opened on 17 June 1901 and was operated by the Great Northern Railway (Ireland) until 1958, when Coras Iompair Eireann (CIE) took over. Tramcars ran the 5-mile route from Sutton station to Howth summit, then down into Howth, terminating at the railway station. Most of the route was single track with passing places, and the track gauge was 5ft 3in, the same as that of the railways in Ireland. For its opening, the tramway had eight trams, Nos 1 to 8, open-top 67-seaters built by Brush of Loughborough. They ran on eight wheels, each of the two Brill 22E bogies having two large and two small wheels, with the motor in each geared directly to the axle with the large wheels. This view of car 4 was taken at Strand Road on 1 July 1958, and the tramway closed on 31 May 1959. *John Clarke*

Rear cover: **BLACKPOOL** It is early morning on 5 July 1958 at Gynn Square, and approaching the camera is No 244, an EEC 'Balloon' new in September 1934. It looks very smart in the livery with more green applied, which was a wartime measure; from 1953 this livery was dropped, and the green was reduced. On this day Gasherbrum I, also known as Hidden Peak or K5, the 11th highest mountain in the world, was ascended for the first time; the first winter ascent was made on 9 March 2012. *John Clarke*

Index of operators and vehicles